Emily Dickinson

"Virgin Recluse" and Rebel:
36 Poems, Their Backstories, Her Life

Lea Bertani Vozar Newman

Lea Bertani Vozar Newman

Shires Press
Manchester Center, Vermont

EMILY DICKINSON, "VIRGIN RECLUSE" AND REBEL:
36 POEMS, THEIR BACKSTORIES, HER LIFE

First Edition
ISBN Number 978-0974638980
Library of Congress Control Number 1-1002817971

Cover illustration by Kelly Kennedy
Designed by Spectrum Design, Bennington, Vermont

Published by Shires Press
4869 Main Street
Manchester Center, Vermont 05255
Printed in the United States of America

To order individual copies of this book or for bulk purchases, write to
Shires Press
Or call 802-362-3565 x171
Or 800-437-3700 x171

❧ Contents ❧

✤ Introduction ✤

*T*he myths and mysteries of Emily Dickinson's life are very much part of the popular culture of today. Questions about her continue to fascinate casual readers of her poetry and to challenge scholars steeped in the study of her life and her poems. Who was this closeted genius who dressed in white and lived an outwardly uneventful life while secretly writing heart-stopping poetry that was discovered in a locked box in her room after her death? How did this recluse come to write sublime erotic poetry while living the circumspect life of a New England spinster? Growing up as she did in a household that prayed together daily, and in a society where Christianity dominated every aspect of life, how did she come to rebel against God and condemn him as a serial killer?

These were the kind of questions that I had in mind when I embarked on the seven-year-long research mission that ultimately culminated in this book. Originally these were the questions I used to lure reluctant poetry readers in my college classes into exploring Dickinson's poetry. Most of them had heard of her although few had read her poems.

I, however, was drawn to Emily because of her poetry, not her eccentricities. Dickinson was not part of my undergraduate curriculum, and somehow she evaded me in graduate school as well. It wasn't until I was teaching an introduction to literature course that I sampled some of her amazing poems in the anthology we were using as a text book. They startled me into submission, and I immediately put her on my syllabus. The students and I responded together to Emily's poems in what became an adventure in reading poetry. I wrote this book to share that adventure with others, especially those who are relatively new to Emily's world, as I was back then.

Emily once asked her mentor if her poetry was "alive." "Alive and kicking!" would have been my response. Her poems live up to her own standard of what poetry should be. She claimed: "If I feel physically as if the top of my head were taken off, I know *that* is poetry." Her poems did that to me. They are viscerally potent. I also found them to be intellectually challenging, often ambivalent, sometimes confusing, and always engaging. I was compelled to read more of her poems and to find out more about her life. Abundant scholarship on Emily was available, and I had plenty of research experience to draw on from my literary studies. I passed along my findings to my students as we entered her poems together. No journey was ever the same; each poem and each class interacted in a myriad of fascinating ways.

Alluring as the facts of her life were, the focus in my classes was on the text of the poem itself. I encouraged close reading and original responses, pointing out that the ambiguity that sometimes perplexed readers was often a reflection of the poet's own conflicted emotions. In each class, I learned as much as I taught. My fascination grew over the years well into my retirement, when I finally had the time to immerse myself totally in my quest to separate fact from myth the better to understand her poetry.

What follows in this book is a distillation of my findings. The initial task I faced – and in many ways the most difficult – was deciding which of her 1,789 poems to choose. I wanted to include the different kinds of poems Dickinson wrote – the erotic ones about love, and the bittersweet ones about renunciation; the blasphemous ones about religion, and the ecstatic ones about nature's beauty; the provocative ones about the size of the brain and the happiness of a stone; the terrifying ones about death, madness and despair; and the fun ones about being "nobody like a frog" and imitating the buzz of the bees. The 36 I finally chose are the ones I found to be most representative of the full scope of her canon as well as reflective of her life.

The approach and goals that inform this book are exactly the same as the methods and aims I established for my courses. The book pairs each poem with its background story — with the people, places, and life-altering events that shaped Emily's experience and illuminate her poetry. It acknowledges the myths that have proliferated about her, but offsets them with the facts of her life by drawing on the more than one thousand surviving letters that she wrote and on the wealth of biographical and historical data amassed by Dickinson academics.

Scholars differ on how much attention should be paid to Dickinson's life when reading her poetry. Some believe it is her interior life and her genius as a poet that is most significant. Emily herself might well have agreed in her day. Early in her correspondence with her mentor, Thomas Higginson, she unequivocally declared: "When I state myself, as the Representative of the Verse – it does not mean – me – but a supposed person." Such a disclaimer is to be expected from Dickinson, the recluse who protected her privacy obsessively. More than 130 of her poems begin with the word "I," and she knew that many of the ideas and the emotions expressed in her poems would have shocked her contemporaries. Her contention that the speaker, the "I," is a fictional creation allowed her to express herself freely without any inhibitions. A century and a half later the need for that kind of protection no longer exists. Direct connections between the persona and the poet do exist in many of her poems. Knowing them helps the reader understand the poetry more fully.

In keeping with this life connection – with the exception of the introductory opening chapter – the poems and their stories are arranged chronologically according to when she wrote them. They cover her relationship with the people who played major roles in her life: her closest friend and sister-in-law Sue, her domineering but loving father, her devoted brother Austin, and her beloved sister Vinnie, who was so different from her. A surprising number of men were also part of her life: a mysterious "Master" to whom she wrote secret love letters; her intellectual equal, newspaper editor Sam Bowles, with whom she shared a wealth of letters and poems; Thomas Higginson, who became her lifelong literary mentor; and Judge Lord, the man she was finally able to love openly in the closing years of her life. The book also provides details on the key events that form the arc of her experiences: a traumatically devastating death watch at the bedside of a teen-age friend; religious revivals at school and at home that compelled her to rebel; a "terror" of psychological proportions that she attempted to hide; the threat of blindness and the excruciatingly painful eye treatments she had to endure to save her sight; and the debilitating grief she suffered after the death of her eight year old nephew Gib, who had been her delight.

Meanwhile, in the midst of each of these relationships and events, Emily wrote poetry however and whenever she could. During the day, she would jot down a line or two on whatever slips of paper were available – a grocery list, a discarded recipe. But it was at night in the privacy of her bedroom that – unbeknownst to her family – she created the bulk of her poetry. Both day and night she deliberately shut herself off from the ordinary social encounters that would have interfered with her focus on writing. As the facts clearly reveal, what Emily wanted most in life was to write poetry. In order to do that, she chose the life of an eccentric and celibate recluse. Relieved of the obligations and distractions that went with marriage, or an active social life, or travel – and thanks to the support of a caring and affluent family – she was free to devote her time and energy to her poetry. She hid from the world in order to write poetry that boldly confronted it.

My book is intended for readers who know a little about Emily and her poetry – and are intrigued enough to want to know more. It can also serve as an introduction for the uninitiated who may have been put off by their initial encounter with Emily's poems. It will make her poetry more accessible by clarifying her sometimes confusing syntax and her unique vocabulary. When Emily's ambiguity poses interpretative questions, I have provided insights from readers whose immersion in her writings has made them qualified to suggest alternative ways of seeing her poems. The commentaries and critiques are intended to enrich the reader's experience. Ultimately, however, each poem should speak for itself to each reader.

For those whose curiosity has been piqued by what they have heard about Emily's life-style and who are more interested in her life than in her poetry, this book can be read as a mini-biography. It is an overview of her life as reflected in a sampling of her poetry. It is also well suited for casual browsing. It can be opened at random at any one of the chapters; each one is devoted to a single poem and provides a rich array of background details that help the reader more fully experience that particular poem.

In the other books I have written about literary figures – Hawthorne, Melville, and Frost – I have always referred to them by their surnames. It is only Emily I feel I know on a first-name basis. Her poetry is intensely personal, but it may also be because I identify with her as a woman. Although women have made much progress since the mid-nineteenth century, I had my own problems with discrimination in the twentieth century academic world. As a result, I have the utmost admiration for this courageous woman who made literary history at a time when women were not expected, much less encouraged, to write serious poetry. As part of the posterity whose lives have been enriched by her poems, I am grateful. I have found my Emily. My hope is that my book will help others, male and female alike, find theirs.

Emily Dickinson

"Virgin Recluse" and Rebel:
36 Poems, Their Backstories, Her Life

1

The "Virgin Recluse" Breaks a Taboo
Wild nights – Wild nights! (1861)

Wild nights – Wild nights!
Were I with thee
Wild nights should be
Our luxury!

Futile – the winds –
To a Heart in port –
Done with the Compass -
Done with the Chart!

Rowing in Eden –
Ah – the Sea!
Might I but moor – tonight –
In thee!

*T*his poem shocked one of Emily Dickinson's editors to such an extent that he almost rejected it – and it continues to stun and bewilder any reader who knows the facts of her life. How did this thirty-year-old spinster, whose protective family lovingly but strictly monitored her daily existence, come to write such an erotic poem that captures the consummation of sexual intercourse with ecstatic abandonment? Dickinson scholars and biographers have examined all available evidence in pursuit of the life experience that might explain how Emily came to know so intimately what physical love-making felt like. They found none. They concluded that she must have been a virgin when she wrote "Wild nights – Wild nights!"

That first editor, Thomas Wentworth Higginson, thought so too. When he came across it among the poems that were discovered in a locked box in the poet's room after her death, he wrote to his co-editor:

> One poem only I dread a little to print – that wonderful 'Wild Nights,' – lest the malignant read into it more than that virgin recluse ever dreamed of putting there.

The poem is totally out of keeping with the "virgin recluse" that Higginson had come to know during the twenty-four years he had been her mentor and regular correspondent. This is the woman who claimed in one of her letters to him, "My life has been too simple and stern to embarrass any." In spite of Higginson's reservations, he decided to publish the poem, but he had just cause to be concerned. Most readers would see it as a candid expression of intense desire for sexual union, with complete disregard for the taboo on such subjects in Dickinson's day. Higginson concluded that Emily's secret lover was totally a figment of her imagination.

The "Master" Letters Connection

Subsequent research made a compelling discovery that shed new light on Emily's erotic experience, real or imagined. A series of three letters in draft form addressed to an unnamed "Master" have surfaced. They may raise more questions than they answer, and final drafts have never been found. They are, however, clearly love letters.

In the first letter, Emily observes, "How... easy quite, to

love." The second one describes the emotion she feels: "A love so big it scares her," referring to herself in the third person. She goes on to plead, "Master – open your life wide, and take me in forever." This entreaty bears a striking resemblance to how the speaker in the poem asks her lover if she could "moor" in him after "rowing" the wide expanse of the sea. "Wild nights" and the second letter are both dated by the experts as having been written in the same year, 1861.

In the last letter, the longest of the three, written in either late 1861 or early 1862, she says:

> I am older – tonight, Master – but the love is
> the same – so are the moon and the crescent
> – If it had been God's will that I might
> breathe where you breathed – and find the
> place – myself – at night . . . I want to see
> you more – Sir – than all I wish for in this
> world – . . . . Could you come to New England
> – . . . to Amherst – Would you like to come –
> Master? . . . it were comfort forever – just to
> look in your face, while you looked in mine –

Once again the poem and the letter echo each other, both expressing an intense desire to be with her lover and envisioning her coming to him at night. A significant difference is the specific reference to Amherst rather than the mythic "Eden" of the poem – one of several details contributing to the theory that the letters were addressed to a real person.

Trying to Identify the "Master"

Dickinson scholars have not been able to ascertain with certainty who this "Master" might have been, although, unlike Higginson, they do generally agree that he was based on an actual person whom Emily knew. The leading contenders are the Reverend Charles Wadsworth and the newspaper editor Samuel Bowles, both of whom were part of her life when she wrote the "Master" letters. Both were married men. Based partly on internal evidence in the letters and on the contacts the two men had with Emily, circumstantial evidence has been amassed for each of them.

The Rev. Charles Wadsworth emerges as the most likely candidate for the "Master" role. Emily met him in 1855 in Philadelphia, where she heard him preach at the Arch Street Presbyterian Church. She wrote to him afterward, but none of her letters have survived. The only surviving letter of his appears to be his reply to her appeal for help. He wrote:

> I am distressed beyond measure at your
> note, received this moment . . . you have all
> my sympathy. . . I am very, very anxious to
> learn more definitely of your trial . . . I beg
> you to write me . . . Sincerely and most
> Affectionately Yours –

In August 1862, Wadsworth visited Emily. Her poem "There came a day at summer's full" has been cited as a metaphoric rendering of their encounter: "The hours slid fast – as hours will – / Clutched tight – by greedy hands – / So faces on two Decks – look back – / Bound to opposing Lands –." This intense farewell scene in the poem parallels a passage in the second "Master" letter, where she describes herself as one "who never flinched thro' that awful parting." This could be a reference to Wadsworth's announcement to Emily that he would be moving to California. But all this is conjectural. No verifiable evidence exists as to what happened during that visit or to the exact nature of their relationship.

There is, however, a gossip's version of Wadsworth's visit that found its way into a book written by Emily's niece, Martha Dickinson Bianchi. In 1930, Mrs. Sara Colton Gillett told Martha:

"I remember your mother saying to me . . . that Emily 'had met her fate' when she went south on a visit. That the love had been instant strong, mutual, that she would go no further for it would mean sorrow to another woman – his wife." Mrs. Gillett repeated this recollection to Martha in 1942, this time adding "he followed her to Amherst . . . and Vinnie [Emily's sister, Lavinia] came to her, and said 'Emily, Emily that man is here!'" Martha's retelling in her book *The Life and Letters of Emily Dickinson* provided a few more dramatic details: " . . . Sue [Martha's mother] looked up from her sewing to see Lavinia, pallid and breathless from running, who grasped her wrist with hurrying hand, urging: 'Sue, come! That man is here! – Father and Mother are away, and I am afraid Emily will go away with him!'"

Such was the general obsession with "explaining" Emily's erotic poetry that such an extreme unsubstantiated tale could find its way into print! Without any hard evidence as to the identity of Emily's "Master," he could just as probably have been another man entirely, someone for whom we have no surviving documentation. Or according to one psychoanalytical critic, Emily may have been unable to distinguish between fantasy and reality: as real as "Master" may have been to her, he may never have existed.

To complicate the issue even further, several readers have proposed the possibility that "Master" is a woman. They see the speaker assuming the role of the male lover, acting as the phallic force that enters the passive, receptive female. Their explanation for this role reversal is that the "I" and "thee" of the poem are both women and are not constrained by any predefined roles or set sexual functions. The most likely candidate for Emily's homo-erotic partner (assuming there was one) is Susan Gilbert Dickinson, her best friend, who married her brother and to whom she wrote what have been described as passionate and erotic letters. From a gay studies/feminist perspective, they are deemed to be of greater significance to "Wild nights" than the "Master" letters.

Attending to the Poem Itself

However fascinating the relationship between Emily's life and her poetry may be, ultimately it is the poetry that counts. A close reading of the poem itself provides its own insights. For example, the poet's use of the word "luxury" in the opening verse sets the erotic tone. According to the dictionary that Dickinson used regularly, "luxury" means "voluptuousness in the gratification of appetite . . . lust," making it an apt and telling word choice. Dickinson goes on to use the imagery of being "moored" in her lover as a ship at sea is "moored" in a port to capture the sensual union of coitus. Extending the nautical metaphor, she is rowing toward the safe harbor that is her lover, where she will be contained by him in blissful ecstasy, the winds now futile, the compass and chart no longer necessary. She knows where she wants to be and needs no more navigating devices to help her find her destination.

Attention to her choice of tense is also revealing. Dickinson uses the subjunctive mood ("Were I . . . Might I"), suggesting that she is writing hypothetically about a possibility she desires. The attentive reader will note the use of the plural form of "Wild nights," thereby gaining insight into the enduring nature of the relationship that she longs for.

In the final analysis, enriching as the biographical conjectures are, it is Dickinson's ability to engage the reader's sensibilities in her erotic experience – physical or imagined – that makes this one of her most effective – and most notorious – poems.

2

A Sister Like No Other

One sister have I in the house (1852)

One Sister have I in the house –
And one a hedge away.
There's only one recorded –
But both belong to me.

One came the road that I came –
And wore my last year's gown –
The other, as a bird her nest
Builded our hearts among.

She did not sing as we did –
It was a different tune –
Herself to her a music
As Bumble bee of June.

Today is far from childhood,
But up and down the hills,
I held her hand the tighter –
Which shortened all the miles –

And still her hum
The years among,
Deceives the Butterfly;
And in her Eye
The Violets lie,
Mouldered this many May –

I spilt the dew,
But took the morn −
I chose this single star
From out the wide night's numbers −
Sue − forevermore!

*I*n 1852 Emily was twenty-two years old and "in love" with her best friend, Susan Gilbert. In April she wrote a letter to Susan declaring her love: "I think of love and you and my heart grows full and warm and my breath stands still . . . " Two months later, in anticipation of the end of their year-long separation, Emily goes on to write:

> And now how soon shall I have you,
> shall hold you in my arms; you will forgive
> the tears, Susie, they are so glad to come . .
> . I need you more and more . . . every day
> that you stay away − I miss my biggest heart:
> my own goes wandering round and calls for
> Susie − my heart is full of you, none other
> than you is in my thoughts. . . and I add a
> kiss, shyly, lest there is somebody there.
> Don't let them see you, will you Susie?

A Rude Awakening

Less than a year later, Emily discovered that her beloved "Susie" had become secretly engaged to her brother, Austin. However shocking this revelation may have been initially, by February 1853 she had accepted her new role as Susan's future sister-in-law. She had always adored her older brother, and she soon became a "facilitating confidante," along with her sister, Lavinia, in keeping the three-year-long secret engagement from their parents.

In Emily's first letter to Susan, back in 1850, she had referred to her new friend as sister repeatedly. Eight years later, in one of Emily's earliest – and most clearly biographical – poems, she validates her early assertion of Susan as sister by placing her on a par with her biological sister, Lavinia. By the time she wrote "One Sister have I in the house," Susan had become her sister-in-law, and in it, she claims them equally as sisters. "They both belong to me," she asserts, but the poem is clearly a jubilant tribute to Sue, her "other" sister, foreshadowing the life-long admiration and devotion she would continue to feel for her – in spite of the differences in their personalities and lifestyles. But it is not a rejection of her biological sister, Vinnie. Emily called the bond she shared with Vinnie "early, earnest, indissoluble." She uses strikingly similar imagery in a letter to Sue describing their indestructible relationship: "The tie between us is very fine, but a Hair never dissolves." (She signed the note: "Lovingly, Emily.") Vinnie and Sue were never in competition with each other because the roles they played in Emily's life were as distinct as each was from the other.

The Blood Sister

The first six lines of this poem are about Lavinia, the officially "recorded" sister who grew up along side of her. Like many younger sisters, she wore Emily's "last year's gown." Neither Vinnie nor Emily ever married. They had a loving relationship, which grew stronger over the lifetimes they lived together in their parents' home. Because Vinnie took on the responsibility of running the household, Emily was relieved of the routine housekeeping chores she detested. She and Vinnie were drastically different from each other. In a letter to Joseph Lyman, who knew them both well, Emily confided:

It is weird and so vastly mysterious, [Vinnie]
sleeps by my side . . . and the tie is quite
vital; yet if we had come up for the first time
from two wells where we had hitherto been
bred her astonishment would not be greater
at some things I say.

The Soul Sister

The "other" sister of the poem was the opposite of Vinnie. Sue was Emily's intellectual equal, and she would never have been astonished by anything Emily might say. They had been writing to each other since their much younger days ("Today is far from childhood"), but their friendship had only grown closer ("I held her hand the tighter") when "all the miles" between them had been "shortened." Sue no longer lived far away, because when she married Emily's brother, the newlyweds moved into the Evergreens, the home that Edward Dickinson built for his son and his new wife, a "hedge away" from the Homestead, the Dickinson family home. Much to Emily's delight, her new sister became her next-door neighbor.

Sue was still the outsider, however. She sang "a different tune," sure of herself and her "music." By the time Emily wrote this poem, she and Sue were both twenty-eight years old, and Emily, who had started sharing her poetry with Sue five years earlier, was still sending her poems, seeking her guidance and response. Yet, according to the poem, Sue – unlike Emily – remains independent and self-sufficient. She can even be aloof, absorbed by her separate past and her interior life: "in her Eye/ the Violets lie, / Mouldered." She is inexplicable and unpredictable: "her hum . . . deceives."

A Prophetic Poem

But in spite of these off-putting shortcomings, Emily accepts her as she is. The poem is a pledge of allegiance to her sister-in-law. The closing line: "Sue – forevermore!" proved prophetic. For the rest of Emily's life, Sue remained her most consistent reader. Emily sent her a total of 276 poems, many more than she shared with anyone else and almost three times as many as she sent to Thomas Higginson, whom she claimed as her mentor. Sue was the only one who ever succeeded in getting Emily to change one of her poems. In spite of some serious disagreements over the years, Sue was still the "single star / From out the wide night's numbers" that Emily had chosen for herself.

Bitter Resentments

The publication history of this poem is a shocking reminder of the emotional upheavals that can tear apart the most seemingly amicable family relationships. This poem was deliberately left out of the first, second, and third collections of Emily's poetry that were published after her death. The co-editor of these first editions was Mabel Loomis Todd, originally a friend of Sue and Austin's, who became friendly with Lavinia. She also greatly admired Emily. After Emily's death, Lavinia was determined to get her sister's poetry published, and when she couldn't get Sue to help her, she turned to Mabel, who was instrumental in getting Higginson to agree to co-edit and arrange for publication. Mabel had the task of assembling the original manuscripts. In the case of this poem, Emily had sent the original to Sue, but she also made a fair copy of it and saved it in one of her fascicles, the packets of poems that she sewed together and kept in a locked box in her room.

Mabel inked over the fascicle copy of the poem so as to render it illegible and never included it in any of the collections she edited. She did so, according to her daughter, Millicent Todd Bingham, out of respect for Austin's wishes that the name of his wife be omitted from Emily's writings. At the time when Mabel began editing Emily's poetry, what almost everybody knew, but what the Dickinson family refused to acknowledge publicly, was that Austin and Mabel had been lovers for close to a decade. Sue's marriage was fraught with bitterness and tension, which affected her relationship with her husband's sisters as well, especially since they accepted Mabel as a friend of the family.

Published at Last

It was not until 1914, after both Austin and Sue had died, that their daughter, Martha Dickinson Bianchi, published this poem in a collection of Emily's writings that featured the poems and letters Emily had sent to Sue. Bianchi wanted to restore for the record the close friendship her mother and Sue had shared over the years. The beginnings of that crucial relationship are clearly revealed in this poem, one of Emily's earliest.

God as a Serial Killer

I never lost as much but twice (1858)

I never lost as much but twice –
And that was in the sod.
Twice have I stood a beggar
Before the door of God!

Angels – twice descending.
Reimbursed my store –
Burglar! Banker – Father!
I am poor once more!

*E*mily was thirteen years old when she first confronted death head on. She was part of the death-watch at the bedside of her classmate Sophia Holland. Sophia and Emily had attended Amherst Academy together. In keeping with the custom of the time, Emily was there to say her final farewell to her dear friend.

When the dying girl became delirious, the doctor ordered Emily to leave. But Emily resisted: "It seemed to me I should die too if I could not be permitted to watch over her or even look at her face." The experience made her ill, and her father sent her away to recuperate with cousins in Boston and Worcester.

A full two years later Emily was still thinking about this traumatic experience – and writing about it to a friend:

I have never lost but one friend near my age
& with whom my thoughts & her own were
the same. . . . after she was laid in her coffin
& I felt I could not call her back again I gave
way to a fixed melancholy. I told no one the
cause of my grief, though it was gnawing at
my very heart strings.

The Second Loss

In 1850, four years after Emily wrote about her "fixed
melancholy" over Sophia's death, she once again came face to
face with death and its aftermath. Leonard Humphrey, Emily's
tutor and friend, died after a brief illness at the age of twenty-six.
He had come to Emily's school, Amherst Academy, as its principal while he was still in his last year at Amherst College. He was
regarded as "a young man of rare talents and great promise."
Emily called him her "excellent Principal" and came to know him
well as a tutor and a good friend. She thought of him as her "master" and of herself as his "scholar." Once again she expresses her
grief in a letter to a friend:

I write . . . to-night, because . . . I am feeling
lonely; . . . the hour of evening is sad – it
was once my study hour – my master has
gone to rest, and the open leaf of the book,
and the scholar at school alone, make the
tears come, and I cannot brush them away; I
would not if I could, for they are the only
tribute I can pay the departed Humphrey.

The Final Straw

The third and most devastating of Emily's losses during the
first twenty-two years of her life was the death of yet another
beloved friend, Ben Newton, in 1853. Between 1847 and 1849,

Ben was affiliated with Edward Dickinson's law firm; Emily and he read and talked together regularly. After Ben went to Worcester to pursue his studies, they corresponded often. In a letter to his pastor after he died, she calls him her "gentle, yet grave Preceptor, teaching me what to read, what authors to admire, what was most grand or beautiful in nature, and that sublimer lesson, a faith in things unseen." In a rare moment of candor, she admits he was "dear to me." She reveals her misgivings about his "faith" when she adds, "He often talked of God, but I do not know certainly if he was his Father in Heaven."

Defying the Father

It took Emily five years to distill this doubt into absolute defiance, but when she wrote the poem "I never lost as much but twice" in 1858, her condemnation of God the father was absolute. In this poem, if Ben's God is a "father," he is a cruel and uncaring one, simultaneously both a "burglar" who violently breaks into the lives of his children and steals away their loved ones, and a "banker" who temporarily reimburses their losses only to take them away and leave the survivors bereft.

The references to these three deaths in the poem can be readily identified by juxtaposing Emily's life experiences with those described by the speaker in the poem. The following parallels emerge: (1) In the letter Emily wrote after her teen-aged classmate Sophia died, the opening phrase "I never lost as much but one" is echoed in the poem's opening line "I never lost as much but twice." (2) The deaths of Sophia and Humphrey left her "Twice . . . a beggar / Before the door of God!" And (3) the first two lines of the second verse ("Angels, twice descending / Reimbursed my store") are comparable to how Humphrey helped fill the void left by Sophia's death and how later Newton replaced Humphrey.

Death as a Constant

Dickinson wrote this poem five years after Ben's death, but in her private world, time was a relative thing, experienced emotionally rather than chronologically. She wrote the letter quoted here to Ben's pastor nine months after Ben died. Fourteen years later, she was still thinking of Ben's death when she quoted a letter Ben wrote to her the week before he died. She proclaimed her conviction that true grief transcends conventional time in another of her poems: "They say that 'Time assuages,' – / Time never did assuage; / An actual suffering strengthens, / As sinews do, with age." Her grief over Ben's death – and over the deaths of Sophia and Humphrey – was as palpable to her when she wrote this poem in 1858 as it was when each of them died: Sophia in 1844, Humphrey in 1850, and Ben in 1853.

Another factor that undoubtedly affected her keen awareness of death's recurring devastation was the shocking death rate in her day. Between 1851 and 1854, thirty-three young people died in the Amherst area. Emily would have been aware of these deaths through her family's connections and the obituaries in the *Springfield Republican*, the newspaper she read daily. These three deaths were the ones she happened to know most intimately.

Violently Contradictory Interpretations

The poem that confronts the God she holds responsible for these deaths has generated a wide assortment of interpretations. The extremes are startling. One reader defines Emily's view of her divine opponent as an appalling God who is "a liar, a betrayer, a killer." A radically different reading sees the poem as "an expression of faith, trust, love, and confession quite in harmony with the established orthodox religion of her time." Still another reader takes a middle ground: it is both "a cry of despair and a plea for help."

A financial metaphor emerges in the word "Banker" and in the related terms "beggar," "reimbursed," and "poor." According to one interpretation, the imagery reflects "the Biblical view that God is the treasury of all our wealth, and that He may take from us what He has given us." Other more feminist-oriented critics read the Banker as a target because he is part of the dominant masculine sphere, where males in positions of power operate with God-like qualities.

Parallels with an Earthly Father

In her depiction of a heavenly father who gives and takes away, Emily may have been thinking of her own earthly father, who offered opportunities but then discouraged her from pursuing them. For example, in describing her father, she wrote: "He buys me many Books – but begs me not to read them." One biographer concurs with the view that her father both energized and silenced her. After her father's death, Emily said of him, "His Heart was pure and terrible and I think no other like it exists." Whatever resentment she may have harbored secretly, she was a devoted and loving daughter all her life. He made it possible for her to fulfill her passion to write poetry.

The grim and blasphemous subject of this poem – God as a serial killer – pretty much guaranteed that Emily Dickinson would never share it with anyone. The church-going Amherst community in which she lived – and indeed her own family – would have been appalled.

The maverick academic Camille Paglia provides a final pertinent comment. While insisting on a dualism in Dickinson that encompasses elements as diverse as the Marquis de Sade and William Wordsworth, she also reminds us that "without her struggle with God and father, there would have been no poetry." Or at least, not the kind of controversial –and fascinating – poetry we find in this poem.

Emily's account of her crushed hopes is like the frustration and disappointment any typical nineteen-year-old girl might feel when duty trumps desire – but with a significant difference. Already, several years before beginning to write poetry seriously, she uses the striking imagery of the battlefield ("rolling drum," "weary soldiers," "waving flag") and the metaphor and language of war ("conquer," "victory," "triumph") to describe her struggle. The passage in her letter quoted above also foreshadows one of her persistent themes: the belief that love of affliction can conquer affliction and that acceptance of anguish can triumph over anguish. It's an early expression of a lifelong emphasis on pain, suffering, and loss that would mark much of her poetry.

The imagery, metaphorical language, and ideas that young Emily put in this letter come together in the poem she wrote nine years later, "Success is counted sweetest." In the second and third verses, Emily sets the scene on the battlefield. She draws on the imagery, both visual and auditory, that she first used in her letter to Abiah. The genius of her imagination allows her – with no direct experience of war – to vividly create a battle scene where a dying soldier embodies her own conviction that only those who experience defeat can truly comprehend victory.

Two years after she wrote "Success," her country embarked on the brutal Civil War. Just how much impact that cataclysmic national event had on Emily's poetry has been an issue in Dickinson studies, but recent developments establish a clear connection. For example, one poem she wrote in 1863 at the height of the war's devastation – "It feels a shame to be Alive" – is clearly a tribute to the men who were killed in the war.

Emily's sheltered and secluded life protected her from many of the harsh realities of her time. She herself admitted, "War feels to me an oblique place." But it would be a mistake to assume that she was not aware of the enormity of the war's destruction. Her brother's best friend was killed in it, and her mentor Thomas Higginson was injured leading a troop of black soldiers in battle.

Emily's letters were full of concern for those who were fighting and dying in the war.

In fact, the first publication of "Success is counted sweetest" was part of Emily's contribution to the Civil War cause. On April 27, 1864, it appeared anonymously in the *Brooklyn Daily Union*, a newspaper that gave support services to *Drum Beat*, a Civil War fund-raising publication where three other poems of hers had appeared earlier. As much as Emily resisted having her poetry published, when she had an opportunity to support her nation's troops, she overcame her opposition to publication and agreed to submit her poems.

Giving in to a Friend's Entreaties

By the time this poem was published a second time, in 1878, the Civil War was over. Dickinson was responding to a different kind of pressure when she agreed to have it included in a book of contemporaneous poetry, *A Masque of Poets*. Her admirer, fellow writer, and friend Helen Hunt Jackson had been trying for several years to get her to publish. In 1878 Jackson drew on their friendship as leverage to convince her. She wrote, "I ask it as a personal favor." She finally convinced Emily that her identity would not be revealed because she would have double anonymity. Not only would Jackson submit the poem for her, but all of the poems in the collection were being published without attribution. Part of the book's appeal was guessing who had written what.

When the volume appeared, Emily's poem was placed prominently as the finale in the short poem section. Most of the book's readers thought the poem had been written by Ralph Waldo Emerson. The exception was Emily's sister-in-law, Sue, who recognized it as Emily's because she had received a copy of the poem from Emily back in 1859. According to Sue's daughter Mattie, when her mother mentioned it to Emily, she went "so white" that Sue "regretted the impulse which had led her to express her own thrill in it."

Success on Her Own Terms

Dickinson's resistance to having her poetry published is part of her attitude toward her success as a poet, something she both yearned for and dreaded – the same concept described in this poem as "counted sweetest / By those who ne'er succeed." Richard Wilbur believes that in this poem Dickinson is arguing "superiority of defeat to victory, of frustration to satisfaction, and of anguished comprehension to mere possession."

The same disdain/desire dichotomy arose in Emily's correspondence with her mentor Thomas Higginson. She wrote, "I smile when you suggest I delay 'to publish' – that being foreign to my thought as Firmament to Fin" (or, as we might say, as a fish out of water). But in the very next sentence she admits, "If fame belonged to me, I could not escape her." The result is a state of paradoxical "love of affliction" not unlike her feeling that day long ago at the kitchen sink, but of decidedly more significance than a missed ride in the woods.

Taking and Defying Advice

Safe in their Alabaster Chambers (1859)

Safe in their Alabaster Chambers –
Untouched by Morning –
And untouched by noon –
Sleep the meek members of the Resurrection,
Rafter of Satin and Roof of Stone –

Grand go the Years,
In the Crescent above them –
Worlds scoop their Arcs –
And Firmaments – row –
Diadems – drop –
And Doges – surrender –
Soundless as Dots,
On a Disc of Snow.

*W*hatever else may have been going on in Emily's world, the driving force in her life was her poetry. While her family was aware that she wrote poems, the one person who knew the full extent of Emily's all-encompassing passion was her sister-in-law, Sue. Emily had begun sharing her poems with Sue in 1853, when they were best friends in their early twenties, three years before Sue married Emily's brother, Austin. In 1882, twenty-nine years later, Emily sent a short note across to the Evergreens testifying to the crucial role Sue played in her intellectual development: "Dear Sue – With the exception of Shakespeare, you have told me of more knowledge than any one living."

Asking for Advice

Emily was always obsessively protective of her poetry, but on one occasion her respect for Sue's "knowledge" overcame her usual caution, and she asked for Sue's advice. The poem was "Safe in their alabaster chambers." Sue responded to it with extravagant praise for the first verse. She admired its "ghostly shimmer" and added, "I always go to the fire and get warm after thinking of it."

Sue's account of the unsettling impact the poem had on her made a permanent impression on Emily—so much so that when she later attempted to define poetry, the criteria she established became the effect it must have on the reader's senses, echoing Sue's experience. Emily declared: "If I read a book and it makes my whole body so cold no fire ever can warm me I know *that* is poetry. If I feel physically as if the top of my head were taken off, I know *that* is poetry."

In spite of Sue's enthusiastic response to the first verse of this poem, her appraisal was not entirely positive. She had strong objections to the second verse, which pictured a playful springtime world of laughing breezes, babbling bees, and piping birds. Emily rewrote it completely, turning it into a wintry cold scenario. She sent it back to Sue with the hope "Perhaps this verse would please you better." When Sue complained that she was still "not suited" with it, Emily revised it two more times. Neither version elicited Sue's approval. In her correspondence with Sue about this poem, Emily's wish to please Sue becomes patently clear. Emily writes, "Could I make you and Austin – proud – sometime – a great way off – 'twould give me taller feet – ."

Nevertheless, when Emily included this poem in her first letter to Thomas Higginson, the editor she hoped would become her mentor, she chose to send him one of the versions that did not suit Sue. When she needed to decide which second verse would make the most favorable impression, Emily followed her own judgment.

The Christian View

Readers with a Christian perspective often see this poem as a confirmation of their faith. For Sue and her fellow members of the Congregational Church of Amherst, the entombed dead are the Elect who await their promised resurrection, safe from an awareness of the passage of time: "Untouched by Morning / – And untouched by noon – ." Their enduring patience as "meek members of the Resurrection" suggest an allusion to one of Christ's Beatitudes: "Blessed are the meek: for they shall inherit the earth." The "Alabaster" walls and the "Roof of Stone" evoke the kind of stone burial vault common in New England in Dickinson's day, while the "Rafter of Satin" of the coffin provides some initial comfort and softens the imagery. For the members of the Christian denomination that dominated Emily's social and cultural world, and for their successors, the first verse is simply a statement of their belief that the Resurrection will come, but in its own good time.

The Ironic Readings

Others, however, read the poem ironically. According to one reader, the meek have already inherited the legacy that Christianity promises them; they "inherit the earth" of the grave. Another reader points out that since the "members of 'the Resurrection' have not been raised up," the poem suggests that reality is immune to their beliefs. The "grand" passage of years in the second verse reveals an equally grim scenario above ground in the world of the living. Its vast wintry void is divested of human significance, as frigid as the alabaster and stone of the dead underground – and as silent. The dropped "Diadems" (lost crowns denoting royalty) and the surrendering "Doges" (Venetian magistrates emblematic of leaders who have given up their power) are "Soundless." It is a universe of infinite space and unending time, an uncaring natural world oblivious to the so-called "blessed" dead, with an apparently indifferent Creator. The speaker is "the unbeliever commenting on the deluded faithful." These ironic interpretations see Dickinson's vision as a dire one that scornfully alters and mockingly rejects Christ's beatific message.

Vindication

As for Emily's decision not to follow Sue's advice when deciding which version to send to Higginson, posterity has proved Emily right. Emily's choice has received much praise for its imagery. One reader admires the movement from the linear, closed images of the tomb into the circular, expanding ones of crescents, scoops, and arcs of the firmament. Another finds the closing image of "Dots, / On a Disc of Snow" especially effective: it "expresses in phonetic preciseness and geometric abstraction the qualities of slight matter, minuscule size, and the feel of cold inert insignificance." Emily may have appeared subservient about some things in her life, but she recognized the genius of her poetry, and about that she was fiercely assertive.

The Sexual Life
of the Flower and the Bee
Did the Harebell loose her girdle (1860)

Did the Harebell loose her girdle
To the lover Bee
Would the Bee the harebell hallow
Much as formerly?

Did the "Paradise" – persuaded –
Yield her moat of pearl –
Would the Eden be an Eden,
Or the Earl – an Earl?

*T*he birds and the bees – and the flowers they pollinate – have long been associated with a child's introduction to the facts of sex, but Emily was a twenty-nine-year-old adult when she wrote this poem about a flower and a bee. In it, she chose to ask: "What happens afterward? How will the partners feel about each other after they have consummated their sexual union?"

It's an unsettling question for Emily to be pondering at this point in her life. She was already well on her way to becoming a recluse. She had gradually withdrawn from social encounters, limiting her world to her home and her garden. From all outward appearances, she wasn't interested in the opposite sex. However, she did entertain a gentleman caller that year.

A Mysterious Lover and the "Master" Letters

In August 1860, the Reverend Charles Wadsworth paid her a visit. That visit and Emily's relationship to Wadsworth have been the subject of much debate in Dickinson circles. As detailed in the discussion of the most erotic of her poems, "Wild nights," in Chapter 1, he has been proposed as a likely candidate for the mysterious "Master" to whom she addressed three love letters. She wrote the first letter in 1858, two years before she wrote the "harebell" poem. The more erotic second and third letters were written a year after that poem. Similar bee metaphors appear in both the poem and the second "Master" letter. One enigmatic example in the second letter declares: "Wonder stings me more than the Bee – who did never sting me – but made gay music with his might wherever I did go."

Only the working drafts of these letters have survived, and there is no evidence that she ever wrote final drafts or sent them to anyone. The letters may, in fact, be as fanciful as some of her poems. But since Emily's imagination provided more raw material for her poetry than any conventional reality ever did, the "Master" letters offer some valid insights into the thoughts and emotions she expresses in this poem.

It is the first of her poems that directly addresses the subject of sex. The speaker begins by asking the equivalent of "Will he still love her in the morning?" The second verse turns the tables on the gender issue by asking "Will she still respect him?" These brief eight lines raise three more equally provocative questions: "Did she entice him ('loose her girdle')?" "Did he seduce her ('the Paradise – persuaded')?" "Have they contaminated their paradise ('Would the Eden be an Eden')?"

A Deceptively Childlike Look at Sex

Much about this poem is childlike. The lilting rhythm of the short lines and the simple rhymes and imagery are part of the poem's apparent naiveté. But Dickinson merely uses the deceptive persona of a child-woman to make an adult observation: she raises the primordial question long posed by religion and society about the negative consequences that might result from a loss of chastity. She manages to present a playful approach to a serious issue by drawing her imagery from the garden that had been a part of her life since childhood.

The harebell, a soft-fleshed delicate perennial with clusters of blue or white bell-shaped blooms, was one of the flowers she tended in her garden. It becomes a metaphor for the receptive female. The bee assumes the role of the seeking male. Both are emblematic of how Emily transforms the natural world that she observes in action in her garden into her distinctive brand of poetry. Both are favorites of hers: flowers appear in more than 400 of her poem, bees in 124.

Victim or Vamp?

Responses to Emily's "sex in nature" poem have been diverse, although none have failed to recognize her metaphor. One reader feels it exhibits a "dread of generalized masculinity." Another believes it indicates that a "lover's physical desire for her touched off profound sexual reservations." A third responds with a contrary view: Karl Keller sees the persona created by Emily as a "lovely, lost vamp."

The Pearl as Clitoris or a Moat from the Bible

The reference to "pearl" in the second verse ("Did the 'Paradise' – persuaded – / Yield her moat of pearl – ") has garnered some attention. For Paula Bennett it is suggestive of a clitoral image, while Helen Vendler finds a biblical source. She cites Revelation 21:21, with its twelve gates of Paradise (each gate made up of one pearl) echoed in the poem when the flower "manifests herself (enclosed in her 'moat') as a single pearl."

The Absurdity of Conventional Morality

An upbeat view comes from Nancy Walker, who finds humor in the poet's sexually oriented garden scenario. She credits Dickinson with reducing conventional morality to a laughable absurdity when she imposes her society's morals on the innocent, natural world. Walker also recognizes the rebel in Emily; she credits her with using the voice of a coquette to find a way to express her defiance of the status quo. Her reading offers the reader a corrective stance on a poet too often associated only with death, pain, and depression.

Faith and Microscopes
Faith is a fine invention (1861)

"Faith" is a fine invention
For Gentlemen who see!
But Microscopes are prudent
In an Emergency!

For a woman often thought of as a painfully shy home-bound spinster robed in virginal white, Emily Dickinson managed to have a series of close and lasting relationships with several men during the course of her life. One of the most flamboyant of her gentlemen friends was Samuel Bowles, the successful editor of the *Springfield Republican*, the newspaper Emily read "every night."

Emily met Sam in 1856 through her brother, Austin, and his wife, Sue. Sam was one of their best friends and a frequent visitor at the Evergreens, their home next door to the Dickinson Homestead.

Good Times Next Door
Sam Bowles was young, good-looking, intelligent, and fun. He often dropped in at the Evergreens unexpectedly, and Sue would go next door to let Emily know Sam had arrived. Emily would join them, bringing with her some of her homemade currant or berry wine. Bowles told Austin that Emily "never forgets my spiritual longings," referring to her "double 'spirituality'" –

the alcoholic spirits and their discussions about immortality and heaven. Emily remembered with pleasure those visits "in Sue's Drawing Room" when we were "talking and laughing there."

A family anecdote captures the camaraderie that characterized their friendship. According to Emily's sister, Lavinia:

> Once, when he had driven from Springfield
> to see her, she refused to come down from
> some whim, and he ran part-way up the
> stairs calling, "Emily, Emily, you rascal! –
> come down here!" And when she finally did,
> the call was more electric than ever.

Bowles was one of the few who made it into Emily's close and closed circle of friends.

Dickinson scholars disagree as to the nature of that relationship. Several believe that he played a major role in Emily's emotional life and that he was the mysterious "Master" to whom Dickinson wrote several love letters, drafts of which were found with her papers after her death. Others believe they were simply good friends on the basis of mutual interests and as evidenced by the many letters they wrote to each other.

A Correspondence Filled with Poetry

Whatever their relationship, Emily respected and admired Bowles enough to share thirty-seven of her poems with him. She was wary about having her poetry published in Bowles' newspaper, or for that matter anywhere, but nevertheless she included her poetry in her letters to him. We don't know how or whether he commented on her poems, because Bowles' letters to her were destroyed when, fulfilling Emily's wishes, her sister burned all of his letters to her after her death. Her letters to him are often as enigmatic as her poetry.

In 1861, Emily wrote a letter to Sam that included the poem "Faith is a fine invention." The letter begins with the two words "Thank you" followed by the poem, but none of the extensive Dickinson scholarship has been able to identify what prompted the thanks. We do know that in the same year Emily sent him this poem about faith and microscopes, Bowles experienced a series of physical collapses that forced him to take several leaves from work. Although he attempted to joke about his afflictions, calling them his "boils & bowels & sciatica," he was seriously ill. Emily apparently responds to Bowles in kind. In these superficially flippant four lines, she undermines the religious outlook of her day and shares her blasphemous thoughts with the man she accepts as an intellectual equal.

Bowles was a secular man, a rational Unitarian unconcerned with theological matters. Emily must have known this, because as a rule the poems she chose to send him were not of a religious nature. This poem is an exception. Emily must also have been aware of Bowles' persistently optimistic outlook in the face of his chronic health problems. He was given to expressing his confidence in "Patience and Faith," declaring in a letter to Austin and Sue, "Faith I find grows larger and richer with me as I myself grow more powerless." In spite of the poem's light-hearted mocking tone, it could well have been a call to action to her friend, alerting him to turn to science for help in the face of his medical "Emergency."

Religion and Science: Friends or Foes

Such an interpretation may explain why Emily sent Bowles this poem, but it gives us only a glimpse into her own attitude toward religion and science. While a student at Amherst Academy, Emily had a strong grounding in science along with the standard theological fare. The rigorous curriculum included botany, geology, and algebra, and it offered the opportunity to attend lectures at Amherst College, where the prominent geologist, theologian, and educator Edward Hitchcock was a frequent speaker. Emily also read Hitchcock's books, but apparently with a skeptical eye because he consistently portrayed science as a supportive adjunct to religion, not as its opposition. Emily's doubts, however cleverly expressed, are evident here.

The "Rascal" at Work with Wordplay

It is this wit and independence of thought that mark the poem as typical Dickinson. Juxtaposing a generalization (faith) with a specific object (the microscope), the poet creates a playful word game with an unorthodox viewpoint guaranteed to shock her contemporaries. By equating the two and classifying faith in the same invention category as the microscope, the poem portrays both the microscope and faith as instruments of seeing devised by humans. It suggests that, in a crisis, science – not religion – might be the more "prudent" alternative. Bowles knew Emily well when he called her his "rascal."

8

Making Merry with Bumblebees

Come slowly – Eden! (1861)

Come slowly – Eden!
Lips unused to Thee –
Bashful – sip thy Jessamines –
As the fainting Bee –

Reaching late his flower,
Round her chamber hums –
Counts his nectars –
Enters – and is lost in Balms.

On a Sunday afternoon in the late 1840s, Emily and her brother, Austin, had what she describes as "a merry talk" about bumblebees. In a letter to a mutual friend, she wrote:

> Austin wanted me to say what is their music. So he buzzed like one and I mocked the wee hum they make down in the calyx of a holly hock. I'm sure I don't know much about bumble bees tho' I have seen them a hundred times go thump down on a buttercup head & never come out.

One of Dickinson's biographers notes that the eroticism of

Emily's language and imagery in this letter she wrote when she was not quite ten years old was probably unconscious.

Eroticism No Longer Unconscious

However, when as a woman of thirty, more than two decades later, Emily uses a similar bee-in-a-flower image in this poem, the eroticism is no longer unconscious but a significant and deliberate element of the piece. When she wrote it, in 1861, bees and flowers and sex were on her mind once more, as they were the year before when she wrote "Did the Harebell loose her Girdle." The bee in "Come slowly – Eden" that hums round the flower, then enters it and "is lost in Balms," bears a striking resemblance to the bees described in the letter above: "I have seen them a hundred times go thump down on a buttercup head & never come out."

The Speaker's Disclosures

In the opening three lines of the poem, the speaker reveals several things about herself. In the first line, "Come slowly – Eden," she invites the bliss associated with Adam and Eve in the Garden of Eden to come to her, but she wants the experience to proceed at a leisurely pace. In the second line, "Lips unused to Thee," she admits she is inexperienced in such matters. In the third line, she characterizes herself as "Bashful" – a word defined in the 1828 Webster's dictionary, which Dickinson used regularly, as "modest to excess" and "exciting shame." Yet, in the same line, the shy maiden ventures to kiss her lover with her inexperienced lips (they "sip thy Jessamines," a nineteenth-century variation of jasmine.) So begins the extended metaphor of an encounter of a bee with a flower for sexual intercourse.

An Overwhelmingly Sensual Account

The emphasis throughout is on the sensuousness of the union. Dickinson's imagery in this poem appeals to all the senses

– to touch and taste in the lips that "sip"; to sight and smell in the "Jessamines," a beautiful, brightly colored, and fragrant flower from the tropics. The hum of the bee evokes a response to sound, and nectar has a gustatory appeal. According to Dickinson's dictionary, nectar is "the drink of the gods; hence, a very sweet and pleasant drink." The final word of the poem reinforces the aromatic pleasure of the "Jessamines," a perfume that Emily experienced herself, since she had succeeded in transporting the tropical jasmine to her conservatory in icy New England and had seen it bloom. That closing word "balm" is defined in the poet's dictionary as the "remarkably odoriferous sap or juice of trees or shrubs." It also means "anything which heals, or which soothes or mitigates pain" – adding another tactile image to the kissing lips.

Anxiety and Gender Confusion

As lush and appealing as this sensual encounter appears to be, it also encompasses a sense of anxiety. "Fainting" in the fourth line involves a loss of consciousness and foreshadows the "lost in Balms" of the last line, a climax that has been called "wonderful yet deadly." According to one reader, the poem conveys a "precarious balance between ecstatic anticipation and fear of consuming passion."

Several readers have noted a confusion of gender roles. The persona identifies with the bee who "Counts *his* nectars" (my emphasis) and enters the vagina-like floral "chamber," but the poem opens with a traditionally female invitation to the lover to enter. For one reader, Dickinson fails in her attempt to convey the "male experience of sex" in this poem: Cynthia Challiff believes the imagery is "too passive and feminine to be anything but a spinster's fantasy of the sexual act."

Emily Dickinson might well have agreed with Challiff on two counts: her spinster status and the fantasy element. She had no qualms about identifying herself as a spinster, and she made it clear in one of her first letters to her mentor, Higginson, that her poetry was a fiction, a product of her imagination. She explained, "When I state myself, as the Representative of the Verse – it does not mean – me – but a supposed person." She claimed that the voice that spoke in her poetry was a creation of her imagination. By inference, the erotically charged experience in this poem was a fantasy.

But the majority of Dickinson's readers today would oppose the charge that this poem doesn't work. When Dickinson approached Higginson for advice on her poetry, the very first thing she asked him was "to say if my Verse is alive?" That was what she strove for, and what – in this poem – she achieves.

9

Getting Drunk on Nature

I taste a liquor never brewed (1861)

I taste a liquor never brewed –
From Tankards scooped in Pearl –
Not all the Frankfort Berries
Yield such an Alcohol!

Inebriate of air – am I –
And Debauchee of Dew –
Reeling – thro' endless summer days –
From inns of molten Blue –

When "Landlords" turn the drunken Bee
Out of the Foxglove's door –
When Butterflies – renounce their "drams" –
I shall but drink the more!

Till Seraphs swing their snowy Hats –
And Saints – to windows run –
To see the little Tippler
Leaning against the – Sun!

*E*mily wrote a letter to her brother in 1852 attempting to describe how a beautiful day affected her. "It's a glorious afternoon

– ," she wrote, "the sky is blue and warm – the wind blows just enough to keep the clouds sailing, and the sunshine, Oh such sunshine, it is'nt like gold, for gold is dim beside it; it is'nt like anything which you and I have seen!" Emily's exuberance clearly overwhelmed her, but not until 1861, almost a decade later, did it find full expression in this poem.

A Shocking Metaphor

To capture the exhilaration she feels, Dickinson uses the metaphor of a drunken woman out of control – an image that would have been considered scandalous in her day. She must have been aware of the prevailing attitude toward drunkenness in Amherst. When she was nineteen years old, the so-called "rum resorts" in Amherst were closed after the town voted in favor of prohibition. President Hitchcock of Amherst College declared, "better that the college should go down, than that young men should come here to be ruined by drinking places." In writing her over-the-top fable about intoxication, she was defying the conventions of her time and place.

Emily's rapturous response to nature parallels the exhilarating effect the dreaded "rum" was reported to have on the college boys of Amherst. The "little Tippler" in the poem is addicted to the air and dew of summer days rather than to liquor, but she is just as inebriated as any alcoholic. The parallel between nature's creatures and humans is enhanced by applying to the natural world the unlikely image of "Landlords" turning away their intoxicated customers from their "inns" – but to no avail because, like "the drunken bee" and the "butterflies," she will "drink the more!" The final image finds her "Leaning against the – Sun" to keep her balance, as any drunk might lean against a lamppost. However, her source of light – the sun – is more powerful and grandiose than any lamppost, in keeping with the jubilant tone of the poem.

Similar, but Different

The most traditionally acknowledged source of this poem is Ralph Waldo Emerson's poem "Bacchus." Emily had received Emerson's *Poems* as a gift from her friend Benjamin Newton in 1849, and she continued to acquire and read Emerson's books all through her life. Many scholars cite Emerson as a major influence on her poetry. Certainly Emerson's essay "The Poet" could have served as the model for the speaker in "I taste a liquor never brewed." In that essay, Emerson counsels the poet that "His cheerfulness should be the gift of the sunlight; the air should suffice for his inspiration, and he should be tipsy with water." Getting inspired and tipsy on sunlight and air is a lot like what Dickinson's persona is doing, but her version of being drunk on nature is distinctly her own. Where Emerson's transcendentalism sees nature as a means of merging with the Oversoul (his word for God), Dickinson's merger with nature does not lead to a union with God but to the glorification of the beauty of this world. In Emily's poem, the "Seraphs" and "Saints" in the heavens above look down eagerly and indulgently on her delirious state of happiness below.

Another difference between Emerson's advice and Dickinson's poem is that instead of the customary association of revelry with Bacchus and wine, Dickinson's words – "brewed," "Tankards," "drams" – suggest beer, a more down-to-earth libation. Germany, famous for its beer, is evoked in "the Frankfort Berries" of the first verse, probably a reference to hops from the German city of Frankfurt. ("Frankfort" is an example of Dickinson's occasionally erratic spelling.)

Breaking the Rules

This poem was first published in the *Springfield Republican* without Emily's permission in 1861, the same year she wrote it. The newspaper altered three of its lines to bring it into conformity with what was then considered acceptable literary usage. In 1890, when the poem was included in the first published collection of Dickinson's poetry, one reviewer complained that her verse was as out of control as the speaker in the poem. It was dismissed as "nonsensical" because of its "faulty rhyme and grammar." Today the early objections have vanished. The lack of control over the rules of poetics are now viewed as enhancing the tenor of the poem, reflecting the fervor of the speaker's response to nature, and retaining the ecstasy that accompanied the poem's creation.

Thomas Johnson, whose groundbreaking textual editing first restored Dickinson's poems to their original form, called this poem an excellent example of both her concern with, and her indifference to, rhyme and metrical exactness. The poem uses the "common meter" of the hymns she heard in church during her childhood, but the regularity is broken. On the only surviving manuscript of the poem, Johnson found alternative readings for two lines that would have corrected the irregularities. He concluded that it wasn't that she didn't know how to use meter and rhyme properly, but that she had other priorities. For example, she conveys the swaying, carefree feel of the country dance, the reel, by combining the a/b/c/b rhyme pattern of hymns with the rhythm and the words that fit her imagery.

The editors' changes in the various so-called "improved" versions only point out, in the words of one admirer, the "effervescent magic of Emily's uncommon, uncanny language." Another calls "I taste a liquor never brewed" one of Dickinson's most "dazzling" poems.

10

The Good Little Girl Rebels

Some keep the Sabbath going to Church (1861)

Some keep the Sabbath going to Church –
I keep it, staying at Home –
With a Bobolink for a Chorister –
And an Orchard , for a Dome –

Some keep the Sabbath in Surplice –
I, just wear my Wings –
And instead of tolling the bell, for Church,
Our little Sexton – sings.

God preaches, a noted Clergyman –
And the sermon is never long,
So instead of getting to Heaven, at last –
I'm going, all along.

As a little girl, Emily Dickinson attended Sunday services regularly. As a grown-up daughter in one of the prominent families of the Congregational Church of Amherst, she was expected to continue participating in the family's weekly excursion to church each Sunday morning. She, however, disagreed. She no longer wanted to go to church. One eyewitness account of Emily's open rebellion against her father's insistence on church attendance reveals not only her determination but also how she managed to get her way. According to Emily's sister, Lavinia:

> One Sunday [their father] was for some par-
> ticular reason more than usually determined
> that Emily should go to church, and she was
> especially determined that she would not.
> He commanded, she begged off, until they
> were both weary. She saw there was no fur-
> ther use to talk, so she suddenly disap-
> peared. No one could tell where she was.
> They hunted high and low, & went to
> church without her. Coming home, she was
> still unseen, & they began to get very much
> worried, particularly her stern father. Old
> Margaret was questioned but could not say
> anything. Some hours later, Emily was dis-
> covered calmly rocking in a chair placed in
> the cellar bulk-head, where she had made
> old Margaret lock her in, before church.

Lavinia did not specify any date for this incident, but by 1861, when Emily wrote this poem, she had stopped going to church entirely. She was thirty years old and had no qualms about writing her own declaration of independence.

This rejection of her family's religious practices was a grad-ual process that neither she nor her family could have foreseen during her childhood. She remembers how devotedly she had lis-tened in church:

> The cordiality of the Sacrament extremely
> interested me when a Child, and when the
> Clergyman invited 'all who loved the Lord
> Jesus Christ to remain, I could scarcely re-
> frain from rising and thanking him for the to
> me unexpected courtesy.

At home, the family gathered regularly for prayer each day. Emily recalls her father proclaiming "'I say unto you' . . . with a militant Accent" that startled her. She grew up with the expectation that she would respect her father's wishes and accompany her family to church services.

Excuses, Excuses

By the time she was in her early twenties, she was finding all manner of excuses for not going to church. Her letters reveal how she used her parents' concern for her health as a pretext. She confides in her brother, Austin:

> I am at home from meeting on account of
> the storm and my <u>slender</u> <u>constitution,</u>
> which I assured the folks, would not permit
> my accompanying them today. It is Com-
> munion Sunday, and they will stay a good
> while – what a nice time pussy and I have to
> enjoy ourselves.

Another letter to her brother prefigures the sentiments she will express in this poem almost ten years later. In it she describes how she is continuing to negotiate her way into minimizing her visits to church, this time in order to indulge herself in the beauty of nature:

> I will write while they've gone to meeting . . .
> I stayed to Communion this morning, and by
> that way, bought the privilege of not going
> this afternoon . . . It's a glorious afternoon . .
> . and the sunshine, Oh such sunshine . . . "

By 1856 Emily was openly referring to enjoying her Sunday mornings at home while her family was at church. In a letter to her cousin and long-time friend John Graves, she wrote: "It is Sunday – now – John – and all have gone to church – the wagons have done passing, and I have come out in the new grass to listen to the anthems." The "anthems" she listens to "in the new grass" foreshadow the songs of the "little Sexton" in this poem.

In another letter to another friend the same year, she writes: "if God had been here this summer, and seen the things that I have seen – I guess that He would think his paradise superfluous." Again, her conjecture in the letter anticipates the poem, specifically its last two lines: "So instead of getting to Heaven, at last – / I'm going, all along." Or as she puts it in another poem: "Earth is Heaven – / whether Heaven is Heaven or not."

A Fellow Rebel

Within the boundaries of her family life, Emily's refusal to go to church was a courageous act of defiance, but in the larger community of mid–nineteenth-century Massachusetts, she was not alone in rejecting the Puritan religious tradition. In nearby Concord, Ralph Waldo Emerson and his transcendental movement had preceded her, both in its rebellion against organized religion and in its celebration of nature as a source of spiritual beauty and goodness. Dickinson had read Emerson, but unlike him, she was not concerned with doctrinal matters. In fact, she declared in one letter: "I do not respect 'doctrines.'"

Although Dickinson's concerns may have differed in emphasis from Emerson's, his ideas had permeated the culture of the times and had prepared the reading public for the unorthodox ideas in Emily's poem. It is not surprising, therefore, that this poem was one of the few published during her lifetime. It appeared in 1864 in *Round Table*, once again without her name or her knowledge or permission.

The Critics

More than a hundred and fifty years after its original publication, readers have praised the poem for its clever use of meter, its wit, and its skilful irony. According to one reader, Dickinson adopted "the characteristic meter and voice" of the songs for children written by the hymn writer Isaac Watts while rejecting the traditional teachings of the church.

Emily's wit shows up in the contrast between the two preachers in the poem: the church's ministers with their lengthy sermons juxtaposed with her understated "noted Clergyman," God himself, whose "sermon is never long." In the same way, the apposition of "getting" and "going" in the last two lines ("So instead of getting to heaven at last, / I'm going all along") lightly mocks the delayed happiness of the conventional heaven. The speaker's playful tone is effectively undercut by the irony at the core of the poem. It is ultimately a declaration of the wrong-headedness and inadequacy of institutionalized religion as Dickinson knew it.

11

Being Nobody, But Not Really
I'm Nobody! Who are you? (1861)

I'm Nobody! Who are you?
Are you – Nobody – too?
Then there's a pair of us!
Don't tell! they'd advertise – you know!

How dreary – to be – Somebody!
How public – like a Frog –
To tell one's name – the livelong June –
To an admiring Bog!

"*I*'m Nobody!" is one of Dickinson's most popular poems – and a good example of what her niece called Aunt Emily's indulgence in "elfing it," a way of "having fun with her audience." Martha Dickinson Bianchi, Austin and Sue's daughter, grew up next door to her aunt. In Bianchi's reminiscences, she describes an "element of drollery in her."

Becoming a "Nobody"

Whimsical tomfoolery aside, in 1861, when Emily wrote this poem, she was already trying to turn herself into a "Nobody." She was limiting her contact with others to a significant few. She was becoming increasingly homebound, having paid her last social visit away from Amherst the year before. She had stopped attending

Sunday church services with her family, and she had begun retiring upstairs to her room when guests came to call at the Homestead.

She was on the cusp of her most productive years as a poet, entering an inner life that had no room for indiscriminate socializing. She admits to her cousin Louise Norcross, one of the few she did make time for, that she is prone to saying "no." When she learns that a visit from Louise would be postponed, she writes: "Odd, that I, who say 'No' so much, cannot bear it from others. Odd, that I, who run from so many, cannot brook that one turn from me."

A Comic Poem with a Serious Edge

Assuming the voice of a childlike persona, the poem is deliberately comic, with a light, mocking touch, incorporating the shy self-deprecating Yankee humor that simultaneously ridicules and empowers itself. The target of the satire in the closing lines of the poem could have been the politicians who were often guests of her politically active father at the Homestead. Or she might have been poking fun at some of the boring and long-winded ministers she heard preach each Sunday before she stopped attending church. Such an astute observer as Emily would have detected the same kind of frog-like inflated self-importance in both. The final image in the poem – "an admiring Bog" – applies equally well to the electorate as to the congregation. She does all this in a simple-appearing poem of eight short lines.

Even as the poem appears to be self-effacing and a plea for silence ("Don't tell!"), the implication is that the "Nobody" in the poem – and the reader she is trying to recruit – are the real "elect," the truly superior ones. It is ultimately a self-affirming poem written by a poet who said of herself, "there is always one thing to be grateful for – that one is one's self & not somebody else."

A Source or a Satiric Foil?

Her early biographer Richard B. Sewall found a "likely"

source for this poem in an effusive poem written by Charles Mackay titled "Little Nobody." Emily could have read it in the January 23, 1858, edition of the *Springfield Republican*, the newspaper that the Dickinson family subscribed to regularly and that she read on a daily basis. Although Mackay uses the phrases "I'm but little Nobody" and "Who would be a Somebody?" Dickinson's "I'm Nobody" is nothing like his overblown, blustery, twenty-four-line ovation full of thunder and lightning. His poem may have prompted her to write her "Nobody" poem, but not as a model to copy. Rather, it serves as a satiric foil to his pompous grandstanding. Her poem is brief and simple and witty, as unprepossessing as its persona, whose declared motive is to remain unimportant and anonymous.

A Harbinger of a Lifestyle All Her Own

This poem could be a subtle early defense of her refusal to publish. The persona's disdain of "telling one's name" parallels Emily's insistence – on the rare occasions when she agreed to publication – that the poems appear either anonymously or under a pseudonym. It could also be a justification for what was gradually becoming her isolated way of life. Although she invites the reader to be a "nobody" with her, there is no record of her ever having shared this poem with anyone. For all of its light-hearted fun, Emily's "Nobody" poem heralded the beginning of what some would call a lifelong self-exile into her own private world.

12

The Bird of Hope

Hope is the thing with feathers (1862)

"Hope" is the thing with feathers –
That perches in the soul –
And sings the tune without the words –
And never stops – at all –

And sweetest – in the Gale – is heard –
And sore must be the storm –
That could abash the little Bird
That kept so many warm –

I've heard it in the chillest land –
And on the strangest Sea –
Yet – never – in Extremity,
It asked a crumb – of me.

As early as 1853, Emily Dickinson was associating the song of a bird with a sense of loss. In a letter to her brother, Austin, who was away at Harvard, she wrote: "Somehow I am lonely lately . . . when morning comes and the birds sing, they don't seem to make me so happy as they used to. I guess it's because you are gone . . . I wish you were at home." Nine years later, at a time of crisis in her life, she transformed this winged, melodious creature into a metaphor for hope, seeking solace from greater woes than simply missing her brother. In her "Hope" poem she created one of her most memorable images – and one of her best-loved poems.

The year that Emily wrote this poem – 1862 – was a difficult one for her. In the words of this poem, it was a time of "Extremity." She assigned a "terror" in her life that had begun in September of the year before, and that she wrote about to Higginson in April 1862. She was, she declared, still "afraid." Just a few months earlier, in late 1861, she had written her most emotionally charged "Master" letter, the last of the three addressed to an unnamed someone with whom she was passionately in love. Whether or not she ever actually sent them, they are evidence of an overwhelming desire that possessed her and that was never reciprocated.

The Disruption of Two Crucial Friendships

One of her biographers describes her as overwhelmed by a "sense of isolation, abandonment, and rejection" at this time of her life; she "felt deserted by everyone who was dearest and could understand her, and on whom she most depended."

Her diminished relationship with her close friend and confidante Samuel Bowles was one of these deeply felt losses. They had been exchanging letters regularly, and she had shared some of her poems with him. But in February 1861, Bowles suffered "a violent attack of sciatica" that severely curtailed his activities and sent him traveling off in search of cures. His correspondence with Emily was put on hold, and they had little contact with each other, temporarily eliminating one of the few kindred spirits she counted on in her life at this time. (The "hope" this poem celebrates proved valid, because the following year their letter writing began anew, and she wrote more letters to him than ever before.)

The other important person in her life that she felt cut off from at this time was her closest friend and sister-in-law, Sue. In June 1861, Sue gave birth to a baby boy, Ned. Her new maternal responsibilities left her with little time for Emily. An apologetic note Sue sent Emily a few months later confirms how much Emily had suffered as a result of Sue's neglect. Sue wrote:

> I send you this, lest I should seem to have turned away from a kiss – If you have suffered this past Summer – I am sorry . . . I . . . bear a sorrow that I never uncover – If a nightingale sings with her breast against a thorn, why not we? . . . When I can, I shall write.

Hope in the Midst of Woe

Sue's sincere regrets and concern surely assuaged Emily's feeling of abandonment and offered hope that their friendship would remain a constant in her life. Her note, with its question – "If a nightingale sings with her breast against a thorn, why not we?" – uses the same bird metaphor for hope that provides the central image of Emily's poem.

The metaphor's origin, however, can be found in a bird poem that Emily wrote for Sue seven years earlier under circumstances that bear an uncanny resemblance to their break in 1861. In the note that accompanied the earlier poem, Emily wrote: "We differ often lately . . . Perhaps this is the point at which our paths diverge – then pass on singing Sue, and up the distant hill I journey on. "

The poem she enclosed, "I have a Bird in spring," is about a bird whose song the speaker enjoys, but who leaves her when summer arrives. The poem ends with these lines:

> In a serener Bright,
> In a more golden light
> I see
> Each little doubt and fear

Each little discord here
Removed.

Then will I not repine,
Knowing that Bird of mine
Though flown
Shall in a distant tree
Bright melody for me
Return.

The bird "in a distant tree" whose "Bright melody" signals hope for a severed relationship foreshadows Emily's "thing with feathers / That perches in the soul / And sings." The visual imagery of brightness and light in the earlier poem is replaced with the tactile imagery of warmth offsetting cold, each augmenting the aural imagery of the bird's positive song of hope.

A Nation in Grief

"'Hope' is the thing with feathers" has a more universal ring to it than the earlier "I have a Bird in spring," which focused on her friendship with Sue. That development could well have been shaped by the devastation the entire country was experiencing when Emily wrote it in 1862. The Civil War had begun, and hope was sorely needed. Emily read the *Springfield Republican* every day and would have been aware of the death and destruction prevalent in the land. She also knew about it closer to home, among her acquaintances. In a letter to her cousin, she wrote:

> Mrs. Adams had news of the death of her
> boy to-day, from a wound at Annapolis. . . .
> Another one died in October – from fever
> caught in the camp. Mrs. Adams herself has
> not risen from bed since then. . . . Dead!
> Both her boys!

In the face of such an unprecedented "Extremity" of grief, hope would be a welcome reprieve – and a fitting subject for an empathetic poet.

Universal Reverberations

Little wonder that Emily's poem has found a perennial place in memorial services and sympathy cards. Who would not find a measure of comfort in the thought that one's spirit can be uplifted repeatedly from within (it "perches in the soul" and "never stops – at all") – and at no cost (asks not as much as a "crumb.") Emily expanded Sue's idea of an injured bird whose singing can bring hope to two estranged friends into a universal concept, offering consolation to all who sorrow.

13

The Light of Despair
There's a certain Slant of Light (1862)

There's a certain Slant of light,
Winter afternoons –
That oppresses, like the Heft
Of Cathedral Tunes –

Heavenly Hurt, it gives us –
We can find no scar,
But internal difference –
Where the Meanings, are –

None may teach it – Any –
'Tis the Seal Despair –
An imperial affliction
Sent us of the Air –

When it comes, the Landscape listens –
Shadows – hold their breath –
When it goes, 'tis like the Distance
On the look of Death –

Winter in Amherst is harsh and cold. For Emily, whose delicate health made her prone to colds and respiratory ailments, winter meant an end to her joyful explorations of the garden that surrounded the Homestead. It was there that she could revel in the beauty of nature, responding viscerally to the flowers, the birds, even the bees – until each year the onset of winter cut her off from that immense pleasure. She was then confined to viewing the outside world through the windows of the Homestead – all the more so in 1862, when she wrote this poem. By then, she had gradually become a recluse. In this poem, she captures her response to a shaft of sunlight that came through one of those Homestead windows on a winter afternoon.

Not Essentially a Nature Poem

For over half a century, in the early editions of her poetry, her editors placed "There's a certain Slant of Light" in the category of nature poems, but Dickinson does not focus on the external natural scene. Her concern is the effect the slant of winter light has on her inner world: the "internal difference, / Where the Meanings, are."

For her, the meaning of the scene lies in its depiction of two of nature's cycles: the annual and the daily. The seasonal year and each day are both approaching their end. Winter afternoons are short, and the light slants as dusk draws near. What Emily sees triggers the oppressive and painful thought of another kind of ending: the inevitable end of each human life, the thing we call death.

An Early Wrenching Experience

The poem's ending, "'tis like the Distance / On the look of Death," may well reflect the poet's first close-up confrontation with death. When she was thirteen years old, a dear friend of hers became ill and died. Emily recalled that event in excruciating detail two years later in a consolation letter to a friend who was in mourning:

> I visited her often in sickness & watched
> over her bed. . . . At length the doctor said

she must die & allowed me to look at her a
moment through the open door. I took off
my shoes and stole softly to the sick room.
     There she lay mild & beautiful as in
health & her pale features lit up with an unearthly – smile. I looked as long as friends
would permit & when they told me I must
look no longer I let them lead me away. I
shed no tear, for my heart was too full to
weep . . . , but after she was laid in her coffin & I felt I could not call her back again I
gave way to a fixed melancholy.

This letter attests to the profound effect the experience had
on her – as do her many subsequent poems about death. This
one, in particular, parallels her early devastating face-to-face encounter with "an unearthly – smile" that turned into the "look of
Death." When she remembers in the letter, "I felt I could not call
her back," she seems to be realizing for the first time the immense "Distance" between the living and the dead. The "fixed
melancholy" that followed is the kind of depression that, as this
poem demonstrates, can come back again years later with no direct cause except by association. In this poem, written almost two
decades after her shocking realization, the "Despair" is "Sent us
of Air," sparked by something as ethereal as a slant of sunlight in
the wintry atmosphere.

A Profound and Secret Sorrow
     "I told no one the cause of my grief," she wrote to her
friend in the letter quoted above, and she asked that her letter be
shown to no one. Her determination to keep secret the depth of
her sorrow stayed with her. To the best of our knowledge, she
never showed this poem to anyone. The closest she came to revealing anything about it is a feeling she described in a letter to

her mentor, Thomas Higginson, ten years after she wrote the poem. In the poem the speaker is reminded of the effect music has on her ("like the Heft / Of Cathedral Tunes") when she experiences a painful response to a shaft of light in winter. In much the same way, Emily confides to Higginson: "These Behaviors of the Year hurt almost like Music."

A Much Admired Poetic Rendering

Readers have heaped praise on her accomplishments in this poem. Richard Sewell claims that no one has surpassed her ability to get at the truth of the landscape of the spirit, the inner life. Yvor Winters believes that the poem's "directness, dignity, and power" raise it "to the highest level of English lyric poetry."

The imagery has been much admired. By skillfully combining visual, aural, and tactile images, Dickinson gives the essentially cerebral action of the poem a visceral feel. As Donald Thackrey puts it, "Light compared with cathedral tunes demonstrates a consummate use of imagery in which the profoundest impressions of one sense are called forth to describe the equally profound impressions of another sense." He also points out that "the final images of sound and sight complete in reverse the pattern created by the sight and sound imagery of the first stanza." The word "heft" adds the tactile dimension, suggesting the heavy "weight of great bells or the heavy sound that great bells create." The editors of the first edition of Dickinson's poetry changed "heft" to "weight" to eliminate what they considered a provincialism, but once again Emily knew exactly what she was doing. According to the dictionary that she used regularly, "heft" carries not only the weight but also the great effort of heaving involved. This connotation carries through to the "Seal Despair" in the third verse, evoking the pressure required to achieve the closure associated with a seal, physical as well as metaphysical.

A Grim Reminder

A final insight into this poem comes once again from Dickinson's dictionary. It gives a dual definition for the noun "slant": "an oblique reflection or gibe." If the word "slant" takes on the added meaning of a "gibe," the "Slant of light" in the poem takes on a mocking quality that taunts us with the sudden, unexpected realization that we are all going to die. The numerous religious associations in the poem – "Cathedral" / "Heavenly" / "Seal" – deepen the despair because Dickinson found no assurance of immortality in the church. Immortality was, she said, her "Flood subject." It is not referred to by name in this poem, but it is evoked through its conspicuous absence; its presence is nowhere to be found in the shadows and silence of the closing stanza.

14

Puncturing the Cornea with a Needle

Before I got my eye put out (1862)

Before I got my eye put out –
I liked as well to see
As other creatures, that have eyes –
And know no other way –

But were it told to me, Today,
That I might have the Sky
For mine, I tell you that my Heart
Would split, for size of me –

The Meadows – mine –
The Mountains – Mine –
All Forests – Stintless stars –
As much of noon, as I could take –
Between my finite eyes –

The Motions of the Dipping Birds –
The Morning's Amber Road –
For mine – to look at when I liked,
The news would strike me dead –

So safer – guess – with just my soul
Opon the window pane
Where other creatures put their eyes –
Incautious – of the Sun –

*F*rom February to November 1864, and then again from April to November 1865, Emily went to live with her cousins Louisa and Frances Norcross in the Boston area in order to undergo a series of eye treatments that involved puncturing the cornea with a fine needle. She had been experiencing increasingly serious eye problems since the early 1860s. In a letter to her family back home, she wrote: "the calls at the Doctor's are painful." The doctor was Henry Willard Williams, a distinguished ophthalmologist who had developed a protocol to alleviate inflammation of the iris. Ironically, the painful treatment was necessary to treat the painful condition that had afflicted her for years.

An Updated Diagnosis

According to an essay co-authored by a medical doctor in 1996, the chronology and origins of Emily's eye problems strongly suggest the diagnosis of iritis/uveitis. A description of Emily by a family friend appears to confirm the diagnosis. "Discoloration and fading of the iris" is often associated with chronic uveitis, and the friend remembers her "Eyes once bright hazel now melted and fused." If this condition is not treated, debris from the inflammation accumulates between the pupil and the retina. It clots and adheres, resulting in permanent blindness. Emily remembered this terrifying possibility as "a woe, the only one that made me tremble." In the same letter she goes on to say, "The Medical man . . . might as well have said, 'Eyes be blind, heart be still.'"

Blindness Imagined

In "Before I got my eye put out," the poet imagines the dire possibility into a reality, her partial descent into blindness having given her a perspective on what it would be like to remember the glories of nature when she could no longer see them. As she reviews them in her mind, she repeats the possessive pronoun "mine" four times, emphasizing the illusory and temporary nature of possession. But paradoxically she makes them hers again through the power of language, recapturing permanently in her poem the impact on her of nature's visual beauty.

She admonishes herself and "other creatures, that have eyes" for complacently accepting the natural world without fully realizing its wonder. Deprivation has heightened her awareness to the point where she can no longer contain it: "my Heart/ would split, for size of me" and "The News would strike me dead." With her new appreciation fully honed, the speaker comes to terms with her limitations, choosing the safer option of seeing with her "soul" while others use their "eyes – / Incautious – of the Sun."

A Real-Life Counterpart

To be cautious of the sun was part of the orders her doctor had given her. She followed his directions: "I have been sick so long," she wrote in a letter to her sister, "I do not know the Sun" and "I have not looked at the Spring." In complying with Dr. Williams' treatment plan, she followed the same prudent advice the persona gives herself when she decides in the poem's last four lines to keep her soul and not her eyes "Opon the Window pane." (The poet consistently spells "upon" as "opon.")

Such a "Window pane" has a counterpart in Emily's life, specifically in her room at the Homestead in Amherst. According to her niece, Martha Dickinson Bianchi, when she wanted to visit her Aunt Emily, her favorite approach was "by signal at her window." That window had become, she adds, "a sort of lookout" from which her aunt could "observe the earth beneath." It could well have been from that window that Emily looked out during the winter of 1865 when she wrote to her cousin Louisa, who had asked her about her eyes. It was February, and her response was "The snow light offends them."

Fortunately for Emily, who never did go totally blind, she did not have to make the kind of literal choice faced by the persona in the poem: to be "safer" seeing with her "soul" or to be "incautious" seeing with her eyes. However, she did make another kind of choice. According to one biographer, her illness reinforced her inclination to withdraw from the outside world. The two trips to Boston for eye treatments were the last she ever took. Another scholar credits her illness with increasing her awareness of her creative powers and triggering her most productive period as a poet. Between 1862 and 1865 she wrote a total of 849 poems – more than in any other four years of her life.

15

A Creak Across the Soul
I felt a Funeral, in my Brain (1862)

I felt a Funeral, in my Brain,
And Mourners to and fro
Kept treading – treading – till it seemed
That Sense was breaking through –

And when they all were seated,
A Service, like a Drum –
Kept beating – beating – till I thought
My mind was going numb –

And then I heard them lift a Box
And creak across my Soul
With those same Boots of Lead, again,
The Space – began to toll,

As all the Heavens were a Bell,
And Being, but an Ear,
And I, and Silence, some strange Race
Wrecked, solitary, here –

And then a Plank in Reason, broke,
And I dropped down, and down –
And hit a World, at every plunge,
And Finished knowing – then –

*W*hen Emily was in her early thirties, she suffered an emotional trauma that she told no one about until seven months later, when she confided in her mentor, Thomas Higginson. In a letter dated April 25, 1862, she wrote: "I had a terror – since September – I could tell to none – and so I sing, as the Boy does by the Burying Ground – because I am afraid –." She provided no further details. She never again referred to this fearful happening in any of the many letters she wrote to him during the rest of her life – or, as far as we know, in any way to anyone else. Whatever it was, its emotional impact was so strong that she was still in its throes when she told Higginson about it the following spring. She writes about it in the present tense: "I sing . . . because I am afraid." Song has long been a synonym for poetry, suggesting that Dickinson is singing (that is, writing poetry) to alleviate her fear. As she says in her letter, she "sings" in the same way a boy might bolster his courage as he walks by a cemetery.

Theories Galore

In the same year that Emily told Higginson about her "terror," she wrote "I felt a funeral, in my Brain," a poem that reverberates with terror. Readers have persisted in wanting to know what that terror was or how it might be connected with this poem. Biographers and scholars have obliged with a plethora of theories. The "terror" could have been her fear of going blind as a result of the eye problems she was experiencing at this time. Or it could have been her despair at the ending of a secret romantic relationship with the Reverend Charles Wadsworth when he moved to California. Or it could have been a profound psychic disturbance.

The Psychological Perspectives

The last explanation seems to fit the thrust of this poem most closely and has received the most attention. One book-length study uses "I felt a funeral, in my Brain" as a basis for a psychoanalytic approach to Dickinson, assigning to her a diagnosis of depression leading to "an emotional upheaval . . . of psychotic proportions." Another book-long interpretation proposes agoraphobia as Emily's mental problem.

A third hypothesis has been proposed by John F. McDermott, M.D. Citing the guidelines in the *Diagnostic and Statistical Manual of Mental Disorders* of the American Psychiatric Association, McDermott concludes that Emily suffered from a series of panic attacks. The "terror" of 1861 represents a midpoint in an emotional chain reaction that began with a description of a panic attack that Emily detailed in a letter to her sister-in-law, Sue in 1854. It happened in church one Sunday, when all of her family happened to be away and Emily went on her own. Although no such specific evidence has been found about any subsequent panic attacks, her doctor's diagnosis in 1883 that she was suffering from "Nervous Prostration" suggests that panic attacks had continued. McDermott cites studies that confirm that "the physical sensations experienced by persons with Panic Attacks are perceived . . . almost always as a feeling they are about to die." He adds that "terror is a word often used by panic victims to describe the fear of death they have experienced." Emily appears to fit the profile of a typical panic attack victim: she applies the term "terror" to her fear in her letter, and she describes, through the persona of her poem, the feeling of dying during the course of her own funeral.

A Fixation on Death and Funerals

Some readers believe that this poem is only superficially about death and have rejected the idea that this poem has anything to do with funerals except as a metaphor for a mental breakdown. However, to dismiss the funeral simply as a poetic device would be a mistake. Death and the rituals accompanying it were a part of the cultural fabric of Amherst in the mid-nineteenth century and very much a part of Emily's world. Any overview of Dickinson's letters or her poetry would quickly confirm her obsession with death.

As a member of a family belonging to the Congregational church, she would have been familiar with the procedure followed in church funerals. This poem follows the same stages: the mourners paying their respects (first stanza), the church service (second stanza), the removal to the graveyard (the lifting of the "box" in the third stanza), the tolling of the bells (fourth stanza), and the burial (last stanza.) Cynthia Wolff points out that what is significantly missing is the "narrative center" of the standard Congregational ritual – the sermon. Dickinson's "funeral" omits this crucial element, which traditionally sums up the life of the deceased and offers the hope of an afterlife. Wolff sees the poem as an explicit refutation of the claims of Christianity. The hymnlike cadence of the verse serves as a bitter irony.

The Visceral Imagery of Fear

What makes this poem unforgettable, however, is not Dickinson's attack on theology but the intensive aural, tactile, and kinetic imagery she inflicts on her reader. She appears to have drawn instinctively on two innate fears that psychologists tell us we are all born with: fear of noise and fear of falling. The poem generates both of them, the first effecting the sense of hearing, the second, the sense of movement. The repetitive treading and drumming, followed by the creaking, build to an overwhelming crescendo of noise until the tolling of a gigantic bell reduces the persona's entire being to an ear. To that terror of noise, the poet adds the other primal fear of falling. The speaker breaks through a plank and drops "down, and down" in a free fall, hitting obstacles "at every plunge." Helen Vendler points out that without the "inflexibility of the rhythm" and the "insistently percussive" meter the reader would not "'feel' the Funeral the persona 'felt.'"

To complete the horror, it soon becomes clear that the persona is dying at her own funeral, raising the specter of the nineteenth century's popular obsession with the fear of being buried alive. Familiar examples are EdgarAllen Poe's "The Fall of the House of Usher" and "The Premature Burial."

Capturing the Uncertainty of It All

Dickinson's celebrated ambiguity shows up in the poem's last line: "And Finished knowing – then – ." Most often interpreted as meaning that "knowing" ended with death (bringing about the end of consciousness), it could also mean that her life was finishing and she completed her grasp of knowledge even at the moment of her death (beginning to understand fully at last.) The final word in the poem – "then" – is equally ambiguous. Does it refer to the time just past when this harrowing experience took place? Or is it used as a coordinating conjunction, suggesting that more is to come and this is not the end after all? The ambivalence may well be Emily's own. She makes a revealing admission in one of her letters when she writes, "We both believe and disbelieve a hundred times in an Hour."

Just as these two conflicting interpretations are equally plausible, the poem's origin remains ambivalent and debatable. Whether it was a rendering of the "terror" Emily revealed to Higginson or a literary exercise describing what it might be like to go mad or to die, the poem was written at the height of her lyric power. As her first biographer, Richard Sewall, put it, "She seems as close to touching bottom here as she ever got. But there was nothing wrong with her mind when she wrote the poem."

Eating the Fellow Raw
A Bird came down the Walk (1862)

A Bird, came down the Walk –
He did not know I saw –
He bit an Angle Worm in halves
And ate the fellow, raw,

And then, he drank a Dew
From a convenient Grass –
And then hopped sidewise to the Wall
To let a Beetle pass –

He glanced with rapid eyes.
Then hurried all abroad –
They looked like frightened Beads, I thought,
He stirred his Velvet Head. –

Like one in danger, Cautious,
I offered him a Crumb,
And he unrolled his feathers,
And rowed him softer Home –

Than Oars divide the Ocean,
Too silver for a seam,
Or Butterflies, off Banks of Noon,
Leap, plashless as they swim.

When Emily wrote this poem about her encounter with a bird in 1862, there were probably more birds in her life than people. She had already begun to limit her physical contact with the outside world to her home and her garden. For her, birds were an essential part of the natural world that she reveled in. She wrote a letter in March of 1854 describing the day as "wonderful" with "the air full of birds." This renewable joy was available with each new spring. Two years later, April finds her "out in the new grass" again in a celebratory mood with the "Robins, just got home, and giddy Crows, and Jays." Among them, it seems, was this aggressive bird that prompted her to put him in a poem.

A Favorite Subject

Birds fascinated her, and they became a favorite subject for her poetry. No fewer than fifty of them appear in her poems. Often identified by name – blue-bird, lark, phoebe, wren – they were species that she saw and heard in her garden, like the robins, crows and jays in the letter quoted above. In this poem, she gives an account of one of these encounters, most probably right outside her door on the bucolic grounds of the Homestead, since she still has a crumb in her hand to offer her winged visitor. She chooses not to specify the species, making her description applicable to birds in general and focusing on the disparity between the matter-of-fact brutality she witnesses and the transcendent beauty birds bring to her life.

A Study in Contrasts

The poem provides a striking contrast between the blunt, straightforward account in its opening verse and the soft-edged images of "motion through space" that close the poem. The bird the reader first encounters, which bites a worm in two and eats it "raw," becomes a lovely velvet-headed creature that flies away as softly as oars dip into the placid surface of a silver ocean and as lightly as butterflies leap. Nature is beautiful and ugly, serene and violent at the same time – part of the "impenetrable enigma" she observes around her.

Playing with Ambiguity

The paradox of the "destructive core" at the heart of nature's beauty contributes to the ambiguity in this poem. Emily uses two other techniques to enhance that ambiguity: word play and disjunction.

In the first two lines of the second verse, she plays with the sound of the words. In "And then he drank a Dew / From a convenient Grass," "a Dew" sounds like "adieu" and "Grass" is a lot like "glass," offering the reader another way of hearing the lines. It suggests a farewell toast before the bird flies away (he drinks adieu from a glass), adding a witty and humorous twist to the image.

Disjunction – disjointedness in the text – is the second technique. Here the disjunction is in the syntax, leading to differing interpretations of the context. The first line of the fourth verse, "Like one in danger, Cautious," may modify either the bird in the preceding line, "He stirred his velvet Head," or the speaker in the line that follows, "I offered him a Crumb." Who is the cautious one in danger: the bird or the human – or both?

Two Different Worlds

Most readers see this perplexing nature poem as an expression of the sharp distinction that exists between the world of humans and the world of nature. Ultimately, the poet can only observe nature, not become a part of it. She may objectively report – with the accuracy of an ornithologist – the bird's voracious consumption of the worm, his indifference to his fellow creatures, and his rapid eye movements when she approaches him. But her attempt to interact with the bird by offering him a crumb is rebuffed. His world is not hers.

She responds by describing his flight to a magical place that is his "Home" – a very different place from her home, the garden where she first saw him. The imagery transcends the everyday physical world to reach a spiritual level, where the elements of nature merge with each other and with time. The air becomes water (a bird unrolls his feathers and rows gently away on a seamless ocean), and time ("Noon") becomes a place (the "Banks" of a stream where Butterflies "swim"). These are the hallmarks of a mystical experience, where all things become one in a timeless spiritual universe. Emily Dickinson didn't need to travel very far from home to experience nature – and life – at its fullest.

17

No Pirouettes for Her
I cannot dance opon my Toes (1862)

I cannot dance opon my Toes –
No Man instructed me –
But oftentimes, among my mind,
A Glee possesseth me,

That had I Ballet Knowledge –
Would put itself abroad
In Pirouette to blanch a Troupe –
Or lay a Prima, mad,

And though I had no Gown of Gauze –
No Ringlet, to my Hair,
Nor hopped for Audiences – like Birds –
One Claw opon the air –

Nor tossed my shape in Eider Balls,
Nor rolled on wheels of snow
Till I was out of sight, in sound,
The House encore me so –

Nor any know I know the Art
I mention – easy – Here –
Nor any Placard boast me –
It's full as Opera –

On April 15, 1862, Emily Dickinson took a momentous step forward in pursuit of her goal to become a full-fledged poet. She wrote a letter to Thomas Higginson in response to his article in the *Atlantic Monthly*, offering advice to beginning writers. Her letter opens with this question: "Are you too deeply occupied to say if my Verse is alive? . . . I have no one to ask – . . . I should feel quick gratitude – ." She made another unprecedented move when she enclosed four of her poems for his perusal. Thus began a correspondence that lasted until her death in 1886.

Attempting to Accept Advice

Unfortunately, most of Higginson's letters to Emily were destroyed when, after Emily's death, Lavinia honored her sister's request and burned all of the letters in her possession. Emily's letters to Higginson have been preserved, however, and provide insights into their relationship as it developed. In one of her early letters she asks, "Will you tell me my fault, frankly." Apparently he did, because she subsequently acknowledges his criticism: "you called me 'Wayward'"; "You think my gait 'spasmodic' . . . You think me 'uncontrolled.'" She thanks him for the "surgery" even though it made her "wince": "I have had few pleasures so deep as your opinion, and if I tried to thank you, my tears would block my tongue – . . ." "I shall bring you – Obedience . . . and every gratitude I know."

Not Totally Obedient

She never openly defies Higginson in her letters, but in August 1862 she admits she has problems following his advice. In that letter she once again expresses her appreciation ("I thank you for the Truth"), but she goes on to confess that when she tries to make her poems "more orderly . . . my little Force explodes – and leaves me bare and charred." Even as she vows "I shall observe your precept," she adds "though I don't understand it, always." In what must have been a response to Higginson's admonition that she should abide by the conventional rules followed by other poets of her day, she makes an unprecedented declaration of confidence in her way of writing poetry. She proclaims, "I . . . never consciously touch a paint, mixed by another person." And she stands firm on not changing what she has written on her own: "I do not let go it, because it is mine."

A Poetic Rebuttal

Bold as that final assertion was, a poem that Emily enclosed with this letter to Higginson was an even more defiant rebuttal to the rules others might attempt to impose on her. In "I cannot dance opon my Toes" she uses the startling metaphor of poet as ballet dancer to make her point. As far as we know, Emily never attended a ballet performance, and she was certainly no ballerina. But she knew enough about the strict, predefined form of ballet to see it as an apt analogy for the "acceptable" poetry of her day. In this poem, she uses ballet's artifice to satirize and ridicule the kind of poetry Higginson advises her to write. When she admits she cannot dance on her toes, she is actually saying, "I cannot write the way you want me to write." Then, in fun or madness ("A Glee possesseth me"), she imagines what it would be like to know how to perform this "dance." She succeeds only in making herself look ridiculous, hopping about "for Audiences – like Birds – / One Claw opon the air," covered with duck feathers ("Eider Balls") and making an exhibition of herself somersaulting across the stage.

Confidence in Her Own Art

By the final verse of the poem, she is echoing the confidence she expressed in her letter. She rejects what she sees as exhibitionism and ostentatious display. Others may have different expectations; they may not know her "Art," but she "knows" it very well. There is no "Placard" boastfully announcing it. She rejects that kind of advertising, just as she wants no part of putting on a spectacle in a gown of gauze with ringlets in her hair, clawing at the air and tossing herself around for audiences. In the final line, she asserts that her "easy" art – subtle rather than flamboyant – is just as "full as Opera," that is, as deep and complete in the world of poetry as opera, the most complex and fully developed form of lyric drama, is in the world of music.

Metrics as a Statement

The poem's meter acts as evidence that Dickinson knew the rules Higginson urged her to follow, but chose not to slavishly follow them. The "dazzling display of varied footwork" in this poem demonstrates that she can write rhythmically regular verse when she deems it appropriate. She skillfully uses form to follow content when she has the meter alternate between three and four beats per line to evoke the dancer's leaps.

A Break in the Correspondence

Emily never received a reply to the letter that accompanied this poem. She wrote to Higginson two months later, in October 1862, asking him "Did I displease you, Mr. Higginson? But won't you tell me how?" and again in 1863: "You were so generous to me, that if possible, I offended you, I could not too deeply apologize." It would be a mistake, however, to assume that the eighteen-month break in their correspondence before he wrote to her again was due to Higginson's taking offense. What Emily did not know until later was that in November 1862, Higginson had gone to South Carolina in command of a Negro regiment to fight in the Civil War. He had been wounded in July 1863 and had remained in the Union Army until May 1864. By early in June 1864, they were once again exchanging letters, and they continued to do so for twenty-two more years until her death.

A Shift in the Friendship

We don't know anything about Higginson's response to "I cannot dance opon my Toes" or the letter that came with it. No references to either appear in any of their subsequent letters. But we do know that when they resumed their correspondence after that eighteen-month break, Emily almost never discussed at length her verse and its technique. She sent him close to ninety more poems, none of them with any significant changes as a result of his advice. Her misspellings, her dashes, her arbitrary capitalization, her near rhymes and idiosyncratic syntax stayed with her to the end. It was the way she wrote poetry – and as she said, "I do not let go it, because it is mine."

18

The Iron Horse of Amherst
I like to see it lap the Miles (1862)

I like to see it lap the Miles –
And lick the Valleys up –
And stop to feed itself at Tanks –
And then – prodigious step

Around a Pile of Mountains –
And supercilious peer
In Shanties – by the sides of Roads –
And then a Quarry pare

To fit it's sides
And crawl between
Complaining all the while
In horrid – hooting stanza –
Then chase itself down Hill –

And neigh like Boanerges –
Then – prompter than a Star
Stop – docile and omnipotent
At it's own stable door –

On June 9, 1853, while Amherst in general – and her father in particular – celebrated the official opening of the Amherst &

Belchertown Railroad, Emily was hiding in the nearby woods. A contingent of 375 visitors from New London, Connecticut, was scheduled to arrive in Amherst by a special morning train to participate in the festivities. Emily's comment to her brother, away at Harvard, was "New London is coming today, but I don't care." A few days later, she provided the details:

> The New London Day passed off grandly –
> so all the people said . . . Father was as
> usual, Chief Marshall of the day, and went
> marching around the town with New Lon-
> don at his heels like some old Roman Gen-
> eral, upon a Triumph Day. . . they all said
> t'was fine. I spose it was – I sat in Prof
> Tyler's woods and saw the train move off,
> and then ran home.

Edward Dickinson, Emily's father, was instrumental in bringing the railroad to Amherst. Without his untiring efforts, that probably would never have happened. He thought the steam engine was "the most beautiful piece of machinery" he had ever seen. He continued to be a passionate advocate for the railroad all his life, literally to his dying day. He was arguing for the Massachusetts Central Railroad in the House of Representatives in Boston on the day he died.

A Daughter's Support

Initially, Emily responded with enthusiastic support for her father's project as she became caught up in the entire family's excitement about the railroad coming to Amherst. Her correspondence with her brother, Austin, traces the trajectory of her responses from celebratory acceptance to what eventually became growing disaffection. When the project is first approved, she writes:

Since we have written you, the grand Rail
Road decision is made, and there is great re-
joicing throughout this town . . . the streets
are full of people talking cheeringly, and you
really should be here to partake of the ju-
bilee. . . . Father is really sober from excessive
satisfaction, and bears his honors with a
most becoming air. Nobody believes it yet, it
seems like a fairy tale, a most miraculous
event in the lives of us all.

When the railroad connection is completed and the trains begin
running, she still writes enthusiastically: "While I write, the
whistle is playing, and the cars just coming in. It gives us all
new life, every time it plays. How you will love to hear it, when
you come home again!"

A Change of Heart

Another letter she wrote that fall reveals some second
thoughts about the "miraculous" railroad. When she reads in the
newspapers about "accidents, where railroads meet each other
unexpectedly," she becomes concerned about how dangerous
and destructive railroads could be.

Not until almost ten years later, however, in her poem "I
like to see it lap the miles" did she express her increased skepticism and disenchantment. By then, she had developed serious
doubts about the so-called progress this symbol of the industrial
revolution was bringing to New England. Dickinson's way of han-
dling her negative appraisal of her father's pet project was to assume a playful tone. As a result, she writes a comic poem that is
a cartoon-like description of the new railroad with some decidedly
ironic touches. Using the commonplace and popular metaphor
of the railroad as an iron horse, she elaborates and exaggerates
the conceit of the galloping horse in the best tall-tale tradition.

A Brother's Prank

A prank of her brother's could very well have been her inspiration for the image of a horse traveling at top speed and returning at the end of his gallop to his stable. According to Emily's niece, Austin's daughter Mattie:

> Austin loved excitement, and liked to drive
> down the Main Street from his law office
> with his horse going at racing speed, reins
> lying loose, turning in on one wheel at the
> old gate, and never slackening the pace till
> the flaring nostrils of the proud animal hit
> the carriage-house door; a bit of domestic
> circus for Emily's especial benefit, should she
> chance to be near the window, where her
> hand seldom failed its flash of salute.

The route of the railroad described in the poem is a lot like the one followed by Emily's brother; both return dutifully home after a bravado show of power. In this poem, Emily merges Austin's madcap horsemanship with her critique of the much-heralded Amherst railroad.

A Riddle Poem in the Spirit of Fun

Emily never mentions the horse or the railroad by name, thus creating what was called in her day a "riddle" poem, inviting her readers to guess the subject of the poem. First-time readers often do not "get" the answer because the conflation of railroad with horse is far from a perfect union. The analogy does not need to be exact because Emily is simply using it to have a bit of fun. In the process, she dismisses the railroad as something akin to Shakespeare's "sound and fury, signifying nothing." Although she had lost her enthusiasm for the so-called progress it symbolized for others, the poem is not meant to be a serious condemnation. It was an opportunity for her to display her poetic prowess in the spirit of fun.

In an excellent analysis of the comic elements in this poem, Charles Anderson details Dickinson's verbal skill at work here. He notes how she uses several effective syntactical techniques for speed: the cumulative effect of the series of alliterating infinitives (lap-lick, stop-step, peer-pare), of the seven "ands" and four "thens," and of the run-on lines which turn the first twelve lines into one breathless chase.

The Sound of It

The poem recreates the sound as well as the speed of her railroad/horse hybrid. What had impressed her originally about the new railroad was its sound — so much so that one version of this poem begins with "I like to *hear* it" instead of "I like to *see* it." "It sounds so pleasantly to hear them come in" she had written to her brother in 1853. But after living with a railroad spur within hearing distance of her home for close to ten years and listening to the engine's comings and goings on a daily basis, it has become a "horrid – hooting" noise.

It neighs "like Boanerges," she writes, which turns out to be a biblical allusion to the name given by Christ to the Apostles John and James because of their fervid and tempestuous tempers. Boanerges translates as "Sons of Thunder," and it has come to mean "any declamatory and vociferous preacher" – connotations that Emily long deemed onerous.

She Likes It?

A final piece of advice on interpreting this poem comes from Domnhall Mitchell, who reminds us that Dickinson begins her poem with a positive statement: she *likes* to see the train go rushing by. It may also be a good idea to keep in mind that one experienced professor, Dorothy Oberhaus, uses this piece in her American Humor course as a comic poem. Dickinson could be saying "If you can't join them, make fun of them."

19

Choosing Friends Deliberately

The Soul selects her own Society (1862)

The Soul selects her own Society –
Then – shuts the Door –
To her divine Majority –
Present no more –

Unmoved – she notes the Chariots – pausing –
At her low Gate –
Unmoved – an Emperor be kneeling
Opon her mat –

I've known her – from an ample nation –
Choose one –
Then – close the Valves of her attention –
Like Stone –

*E*mily always had a few close friends whom she cherished, but she didn't much like people in general. When Thomas Higginson, whom she had chosen as a friend and a mentor, asked her who her "Companions" were, her response was "Hills – Sir – and the Sundown – and a Dog – large as myself, that my Father bought me – They are better than Beings – because they know – but do not tell. " When he persisted in asking why she was "shunning Men and Women," her explanation was this: because "they talk of Hallowed things, aloud – and embarrass my Dog – He and I don't object to them, if they'll exist their side."

Shutting Some Out

The same year that this exchange took place, in 1862, Dickinson wrote what many consider to be her "declaration of independence" from her social obligations. In this poem she claims her right to limit her friendship to a select few and to ignore the rest of society. The process of shutting herself off from life's ordinary social encounters had begun as early as 1854. The following letter clearly highlights how she went about it. In responding to an invitation from Abiah Root, who had been one of her closest friends at school, she sent her regrets by explaining:

> I don't go from home, unless emergency
> leads me by the hand, and then I do it obsti-
> nately, and draw back if I can. Should I ever
> leave home, which is improbable, I will with
> much delight, accept your invitation; till
> then, my dear Abiah, my warmest thanks
> are your's, but don't expect me.

This is the last letter that Emily sent to Abiah, and it serves as an apt illustration of how, with the abrupt and final-sounding "don't expect me," she could, as she put it in this poem, "close the valves of her attention – / Like Stone."

Except for Family

Foremost among those she did not shun were her brother, Austin, and her sister, Lavinia. They shared a unique bond. Other families "are not like us," she wrote to her brother. "What makes a few of us so different from others? . . . It's a question I often ask myself."

On one rare occasion, Emily included someone outside her family in that exclusive circle. In 1853 Sue Gilbert was her closest friend, a "chosen" one, even before she became engaged to her brother, Austin. Emily described their foursome – herself, her siblings, and Sue – this way: "we're all unlike most everyone, and are therefore more dependent on each other for delight."

Watching for "the Rewarding Person"

Lavinia defended her sister's discriminating choices of friends. "As for Emily," she once explained, "she was not withdrawn or exclusive really. She was always watching for the rewarding person to come . . . she was a very busy person herself." Over the years, and from time to time, Emily chose several "rewarding" persons worthy of her attention. When Sue's busy life as wife, mother, and popular society matron left little room for Emily and her poetry, Emily turned to a new "best" friend, Thomas Higginson. During the course of their twenty-four-year friendship, she sent him 71 letters and 102 poems. He visited her only twice, but his account of their first meeting captures the intensity a friendship with Emily could entail: "I never was with any one who drained my nerve power so much. Without touching her, she drew from me. I am glad not to live near her." Apparently, that was the effect she had when the "valves of her attention" were focused on one particular friend.

Another Notable Exception

Another friend Emily's soul selected was Samuel Bowles, whom she met when she was still attending Austin and Sue's evening parties in the early 1850s. Bowles was the dynamic and successful editor of the *Springfield Republican*, and their lengthy correspondence lasted until his death. According to one of Dickinson's biographers, she responded so powerfully to Bowles because she could see her own hyper-energetic states in his driving personality.

In one of her letters to Bowles, she claims, "My friends are my 'estate.' Forgive me then the avarice to hoard them!" In another, she writes: "My friends are very few. I can count them on my fingers – and besides have fingers to spare." Just as the soul, in this poem, ignores the "ample nation" and focuses on a selected one, Emily often concentrated on one beloved friend at a time. Her circle of companions made up in depth what it lacked in breadth.

Unmoved by Chariots or an Emperor

The imagery of royalty rejected in the poem's second verse parallels a choice Dickinson made five years earlier. In 1857, she ignored Ralph Waldo Emerson's overnight visit at Austin and Sue's home next door to the Homestead. Sue prided herself on being a hostess to the celebrities of her day. She called them her "royal guests," and their "Chariots" would have passed Emily's home, "her low – Gate," on their way to the adjacent Evergreens. For Sue, Emerson's visit was a treasured social triumph, but Emily did not meet him on this occasion – or ever – in spite of her admiration for his writings. In the hyperbole of poetry, Emerson could well be dubbed the "Emperor" of New England's literary establishment at this time. The poem twice declares the speaker's soul "unmoved" by such regal trappings.

Identifying the "One"

Although most readers assume that the chosen "one" in the last verse is a special person, two other possibilities have been proposed. The first is that the object of the speaker's sole attention is the art of poetry. The poet Adrienne Rich is among those who believe this poem expresses Emily's total commitment of her life to writing poetry. Rich sees Emily's seclusion as a deliberate choice intended to control the disposal of her time and energy. Such an interpretation is supported by what Emily was doing when she wrote this poem in 1862, which has been called "her most dazzingly productive year as a poet." She wrote more poems – including some of her most highly acclaimed ones – in that year than in any other single year of her life. She had to have been aware of just how exceptional she was and of how essential it was that she let nothing interfere with her writing.

The second possibility is that the chosen "one" in the last verse is God. Who but God is "higher and more important than an emperor," asks Frederick Morey. A marked sentence in Emily's copy of Thomas à Kempis's book *Of the Imitation of Christ* supports that possibility: "The greatest Saints avoided the society of men when they could conveniently; and did rather choose to live to God in secret." In the poem, the irrevocable commitment the soul makes is like the celebrated perseverance of saints.

It is also in keeping with the Calvinists' insistence that the soul should exercise its freedom to select its destiny and then persist in pursuing it. Anthony Hecht expands the Calvinist underpinnings by drawing a parallel between the individual soul and God: "As the soul is to its society (absolute, arbitrary, ruthless) so is God in 'His election and salvation of souls.'"

Rejecting Emily's Rejection

Not all the response to Dickinson's antisocial poem has been positive. To one reader this poem is a display of "astounding pride and arrogance." To another it bears witness to how the soul, by shutting out others, closes in on itself and becomes its own tomb. And according to still another, the poem carries the concept of what Emerson called "self-reliance" too far to its ultimate conclusion – isolation.

Despair or Fulfillment?

In short, three plausible motives for her decision to forsake society in general have been proposed: to focus her attention on a few select friends, to follow her destiny as a poet, or to better pursue and attempt to resolve her quarrel with God. While some interpret the poem as the anguished cry of a lonely, isolated soul cut off from human contact, most readers see it as the bold statement of one who has defied society's expectations and deliberately chosen her own kind of fulfillment.

A comment made by her sister illuminates the extent of Emily's self sufficiency. When Lavinia was asked if she could not get Emily to go out occasionally, she replied, "But why should I? She is quite happy and contented as she is. I would only disturb her."

20

The Power of White

Mine – by the right of the White Election! (1862)

Mine – by the right of the White Election!
Mine – by the Royal Seal!
Mine – by the sign in the Scarlet prison –
Bars – cannot conceal!

Mine – here – in Vision – and in Veto!
Mine – by the Grave's Repeal –
Titled – Confirmed –
Delirious Charter!
Mine – long as Ages steal!

O ne of the myths that has circulated about Emily is actually based on fact: she did dress exclusively in white, but not all her life. Exactly when she began wearing white year-round is not known. Joseph Lyman, a family friend, remembers seeing her in white as early as 1860, when she would have been in her early thirties. Her niece, Martha, who was born in 1866, unequivocally states: "During my memory of her she wore white exclusively, and when the season turned chill, a little shoulder cape crocheted of soft white worsted." Mabel Loomis Todd, who would become the co-editor of her first poetry collection, recalls playing the piano in the Homestead parlor for the Dickinson family in the early 1880s and seeing Emily half-hidden upstairs, "her dress a spot of white in the dim hall." One of Emily's white dresses is still in existence. It is owned by The Amherst Historical Society. A replica is on permanent display in the Homestead, part of the Emily Dickinson Museum complex in Amherst.

While her dressing in white is clearly well established, why she chose to do so is not. Once again her niece, Martha, provides one explanation: she conjectures that "her habitual wearing of white . . . was a sort of memorial to the man she loved, and whom she renounced." The likeliest candidate for this role is the Reverend Charles Wadsworth, who has been proposed as "Master" and as the intended recipient of three love letters she wrote in draft form in the early 1860s – about the same time she started wearing her white dresses.

In 1862 Emily's focus on white extended beyond the color of her dress; that year she wrote three poems that prominently featured white imagery. "Mine – by the Right of the White Election" was one of the three. The editors of the first edition of Dickinson's poetry grouped it in Book II under the category "LOVE." They attributed a lost love theme to the poem, using the same rationale used by Martha to account for Emily's white dress.

Read from that perspective, the poem becomes a triumphant acceptance of her decision to forego consummating her love in this world. The "White Election" in the first line of the poem can also refer to her decision to wear white, the color of virginity and purity. It would be a sign of her willingness to renounce the urges pent up in the "Scarlet prison" of her body; it would signal her "Veto" of a union with her lover on earth and proclaim her "Vision" of their eventual union in eternity.

A very different motivation for Emily's wearing white has also been presented. It could be her way of acknowledging her decision to dedicate herself to the writing of poetry. She could have been inspired by one of her favorite heroines, the title character in Elizabeth Barrett Browning's novel-length poem "Aurora Leigh." Emily's fictional predecessor chose writing poetry over getting married – and wore white. Emily greatly admired Elizabeth Browning and mourned deeply for her when she died in 1861 – about the time Emily started wearing white.

This second approach has garnered majority support over the years. As more has become known about Dickinson's life, it has become clear that she needed tremendous determination to become a poet in the face of overwhelming odds. Her father, upon whom she was totally dependent, disapproved of women writers; her kind of poetry defied the accepted conventions of her day; and her inhibitions about public attention made publication problematic.

But in this poem, she accepts her "Election" to the high office of poet. It is hers, she announces, claiming it as "Mine" six times in succession. That possessive pronoun – "Mine" – is the first word in six of the poem's nine lines, boldly proclaiming her choice. Her "White Election" to virgin poet (the "Vision" in line 5) makes a striking contrast to the "Scarlet prison," the conventional life of marriage in society. She feels herself "Titled" and "Confirmed" in a "Delirious Charter," certified by a "Royal Seal." The "Veto" will be lifted at the end of her life ("by the Grave's Repeal.") It is true that although she asked her sister to burn her letters, she did NOT ask her to destroy her poetry. That continues to live after her death: a "Vision" that will last forever ("long as Ages steal.")

The Gentleman Caller and the Maiden
Because I could not stop for Death (1862)

Because I could not stop for Death –
He kindly stopped for me –
The Carriage held but just Ourselves –
And Immortality.

We slowly drove – He knew no haste
And I had put away
My labor and my leisure too,
For His Civility –

We passed the School, where children strove
At Recess – in the Ring –
We passed the Fields of Gazing Grain –
We passed the setting Sun –

Or rather – He passed Us –
The Dews drew quivering and Chill –
For only Gossamer, my Gown –
My Tippet – only Tulle –

We paused before a House that seemed
A Swelling of the Ground –
The Roof was scarcely visible –
The Cornice – in the Ground –

Since then – 'tis Centuries – and yet
Feels shorter than the Day
I first surmised the Horses' Heads
Were toward Eternity –

*A*fter reading this poem, Allen Tate declared that Cotton Mather would have burned Emily Dickinson as a witch. However, Mather's descendants in Dickinson's time – the good Puritan Christians of Amherst's Congregationalist Church – never had the opportunity to condemn her as a heretic. Like most of her poems, this one was not published until after her death. Today it is the most famous of her poems – and one with no specific biographical connection. It is strictly a work of her imagination – chillingly vivid, written at the height of her poetic power.

What She Knew of Death

Yet, it draws on what she knew personally about death in 1862 when she was thirty-one years old and wrote this poem. From the ages of nine to twenty-four, Emily lived in a house on North Pleasant Street, adjacent to the village burial ground, where she regularly saw a steady stream of funeral processions go by. Before she celebrated her twenty-third birthday, she had been devastated by the loss of three of her closest friends, all of whom died young: her classmate Sophia Holland in 1844; her tutor Leonard Humphrey in 1850; and her "Preceptor" Ben Newton in 1853.

What She Knew of Immortality

This poem also draws on what she knew about the Christian promise of immortality. Whether it may or may not follow death is ultimately the central concern of this poem. She had been hearing about immortality all her life. While she was growing up, her father would begin the day by reading from the Bible and leading the family in prayers. Her exposure continued throughout her school years, both at Amherst Academy, whose stated purpose was to promote "morality, piety and religion," and at Mount Holyoke Female Seminary, where revivals pressured the students to publicly accept Christ and his promise of "eternal life." Until her mid-twenties, when she began to avoid attending church services, she heard sermons each Sunday at Amherst's Congregational Church, one of the outposts of America's Puritan past.

Belief and Doubt

She clearly reveals her doubts about immortality in her letter to Ben Newton's pastor after Ben's death: "Please Sir, to tell me if he was willing to die. If you think him at Home, I should love so much to know certainly, that he was today in Heaven." The absolute certainty she was seeking evaded her continually; nevertheless, she kept questioning. Her letters and her poems are filled with both belief in an afterlife and skepticism about it. Nowhere is her ambivalence more viscerally rendered than in this poem.

The Maiden's Tale

In the first three stanzas, death appears in the form of a gentleman who calls on a maiden to take her on a carriage ride (the original edition titled the poem "The Chariot"). Accompanied in the appropriate Victorian manner by a chaperone – "Immortality" – their journey takes them through a series of scenes that suggest the stages of life. The "labor" and "leisure" that the maiden set aside when she joined him encompass the major activities of life: work and play. The earliest phase of life, childhood, is captured in the image of the school (where children work) and at recess (where they play); the ring in which the children strive is symbolic of the human cycle of birth and death. Maturity is ev-

ident in the fields of ripe grain; its fixed unseeing gaze is a har-
binger of its demise during the harvest, suggestive of the poet's
own lifelong fixation on death. Finally, the setting sun prefigures
the end of the journey, the closing chapter in the progression of
human life.

In the fourth verse, the chivalrous tale takes an abrupt turn,
when the maiden realizes that she and her companions have not
passed the sun. Instead, the sun with its light and warmth has
passed them, leaving her forever in its wake. She feels a quivering
chill and becomes aware that she is not appropriately dressed in
her gossamer gown and tulle tippet (a term used for a lady's
wrap.) The tactile imagery in this stanza underscores how unpre-
pared she was; it captures the shock to her soul as her mind recognizes that she has been deceived by Death's "civility." One
reader bluntly declares: "That obliging gentleman who stops for
her is no wooer. He is the village undertaker." David Porter examines both the grammar and tone of the fourth stanza to show
how the serene assurance that begins the poem is abruptly aban-
doned.

An Inconclusive Finale
The next stanza confirms the grim suspicion that her next
home will be her grave. In stanza five, the house that awaits her
is "A Swelling of the Ground," an image often interpreted as the
excess soil atop a cemetery plot that marks where a recent burial
has taken place. It could also be a reference to a special kind of
burial vault used in New England during Dickinson's lifetime. Ironically, the swelling suggests a pregnancy, but it is a gestation of
death, not birth. The cornice of her new house – the cover of
her coffin – is under the ground. Sinking along with it will be her
bodily remains, all that will be left of her on earth – in earth.
The entire poem is a confrontation between the decay of our visible mortality, the body, and the invisible but hoped-for immortality of the soul. The closing image in the last stanza – "the

"Horses' Heads / were toward Eternity" – returns the reader to the carriage-ride metaphor that opens the poem. The confusing telescoping of time that precedes it ("Since then – 'tis Centuries – and yet/ Feels shorter . . . ") leaves the reader wondering if this carriage will ever reach its destination – or where that final resting place might be. The travel companion – "Immortality" – that started out on this journey with the maiden is nowhere to be seen.

A History of High Praise

The same year that Emily wrote "Because I could not stop for Death," she wrote more than a dozen other poems dealing explicitly or implicitly with immortality. It was, she claimed, her "Flood subject" – and it continued to be throughout her life. In the poetic deluge she created, none have garnered as much attention and critical acclaim as this poem.

An early Dickinson admirer heralded it as "one of the greatest in the English language." In it, Allen Tate, sees an association in perfect equality between the concrete images in the poem and its two abstractions: immortality and eternity. It is a feat she achieved in her distinctive way because, as he famously said, "she sees the ideas, and thinks the perceptions."

Subsequent readers have noted the effect of the pivotal fourth stanza on the poem as a whole, most significantly how it increases the ambiguity of the closing lines. This last verse is a prime example of Dickinson's duality, a demonstration of how her poetry can lend itself equally to opposing interpretations. Consequently, the poem has been seen as both an affirmation of immortality and a rejection of it.

An Ongoing Strggle

Bewildering as this paradox may be, it clearly reveals Dickinson wrestling with the concept of an eternal life for the soul in the face of the physical destruction of the body. She doesn't provide a pat answer, but her poetic genius brings her struggle – her fantasy, her doubt, her fear, her hope – vividly and memorably to life. The poem has achieved an immortality of its own.

22

Writing for Posterity
This is my letter to the World (1863)

This is my letter to the World
That never wrote to Me –
The simple News that Nature told –
With tender Majesty

Her Message is committed
To Hands I cannot see –
For love of her – Sweet – countrymen –
Judge tenderly – of Me

*L*etters mattered to Emily. To her, a letter was a "joy." "A letter," she said, always felt "like immortality," the same word she used to identify the "Flood subject" for her poetry. She wrote an estimated ten thousand letters during her lifetime, but only 1,049 of them are reprinted in the three-volume collection currently available. They were, for the major part of her life, her main contact with the outside world, and she took great care in writing them. They often went through several drafts, just as her poems did. After her death, her sister found hundreds of scraps of paper in her room filled with her writing, some on the backs of grocery lists and on the corners of torn envelopes. Drafts of letters and poems in various stages were intermingled throughout.

A Different Kind of Letter

Emily had thought about her poems as letters long before she wrote this poem in 1863. Thirteen years earlier, she wrote to her friend Jane Humphrey about a different kind of letter than the ones that "go in post-offices":

> I have written you a great many letters since
> you left me – not the kind of letters that go
> in post-offices – and rise in mail-bags – but
> queer – little silent ones – . . . and you would
> paper and ink letters –I will try one of those
> – tho not half so precious as the other kind. I
> have written those at night – when the rest
> of the world were at sleep.

The "queer . . . precious" ones that she wrote at night in her head evolved into her poetry, which she often stayed up late to write, after everyone else in the house had gone to bed.

A Poem Merged with a Letter

Also in the 1850s, Emily actually merged a poem with a letter. The final lines in a letter she wrote to her brother, Austin, are a poem in prose form:

> . . . there is another sky ever serene and
> fair, and there is another sunshine, tho' it
> be darkness there – never mind faded
> forests, Austin, never mind silent fields –
> here is a little forest whose leaf is ever
> green, here is a brighter garden, where not
> a frost has been, in its unfading flowers I
> hear the bright bee hum, prithee, my
> Brother, into my garden come!

A Letter as Precursor to a Poem

At other times a poem will echo a letter. In 1854, Emily wrote to Sue Gilbert:

> I rise, because the sun shines, and sleep has
> done with me, and I brush my hair, and
> dress me, and wonder what I am and who
> has made me so, and then I wash the dishes,
> and anon, wash them again, and thus 'tis af-
> ternoon, and Ladies call, and evening, and
> some members of another sex come in to
> spend the hours, and then that day is done.
> And, prithee, what is Life?

In 1863, she wrote a poem that opens with similar observations about how the everyday mundane routine obscures the significant issues of existence:

> "I tie my hat – I crease my shawl – / Life's
> little duties do . . . / I put new Blossoms in
> the Glass – / And throw the old – away – / .
> . . I push a petal from my Gown / That an-
> chored there – I weigh / The time 'twill be
> till six 'clock / So much I have to do – / And
> yet – existence – some way back – /
> Stopped – struck – my ticking – through ."

As George Monteiro aptly put it: "The often complementary, sometimes duplicative substance of her poems and letters .
. . bear out their interchangeability." In this poem, an equally
clear correlation can be seen between the creator of the poem
and its persona. In spite of Emily's disclaimer that the voice in
her poetry is not her own but that of a "supposed person," in
this poem the parallels between Emily and the speaker are

patently clear. A close reading highlights how each characteristic of the speaker is also a characteristic of the poet:

First, the speaker identifies her poem as a letter, a written means of communicating with others, not just as a private expression for her own gratification ("This is my letter").

Second, this "letter" is addressed to a multitude with whom she has had no correspondence until now ("to the World / That never wrote to Me – ").

Third, her purpose in writing is to convey to others what she has learned from her encounters with nature (the "News that Nature told – ").

Fourth, she therefore hopes her "Message" will somehow get to those who are out of her reach now – to posterity ("To Hands I cannot see – ").

And fifth, she identifies these future readers as fellow Americans ("Sweet – countrymen") whose approval and understanding she seeks ("Judge tenderly – of Me").

The Civil War Connection

Although nothing in the text of this poem appears to connect it with the Civil War, the circumstances of its composition suggest a relationship. As a rule, Dickinson's poetry shied away from political commentary and national events. But in 1863, when she wrote this poem, the Civil War was raging, and in March of that year, the war had become personal. Her brother's close friend Frazar Stearns was killed in action in North Carolina. Emily wrote to her Norcross cousins: "Austin is stunned completely," and she mourned the loss of "this young crusader – too brave that he could fear to die." Her poem "It feels a shame to be Alive" commemorates his sacrifice. It was written the year he died, the same year she wrote this poem.

Evidence that Emily herself thought of this poem as associated with the Civil War comes from one of the fascicles she assembled. These fascicles were fair copies of selected poems on sheets of paper that she hand-sewed together. It was her way of editing and self-publishing her work. She bound this poem in a fascicle that contained two other Civil War poems, suggesting a thematic connection.

Most convincing, however, is the fact that this is the only one of her poems addressed to her "countrymen." She wrote it at a time when she was confronted by the brutal effects of the war and could – in a rare gesture of inclusion – identify with her fellow Americans. Like her, they were affected by the war. This bond prompted her to call out to them for understanding in the context of another bond – her love of nature, whose "News" she attempted to communicate in her many nature poems.

An Instinct to Preserve

This poem offers readers some insight into how Dickinson's reluctance to publish in the face of her fervent need to write can be reconciled with her relentless search for immortality. She told her sister, Lavinia, she wanted her letters burned after her death, but she gave no such orders about the poems she had saved in a locked box in her room. They were not destroyed. Dickinson had taken the first crucial step in the process that would eventually see her poetry – her letters to the World – preserved and delivered.

The Future World's Response

Although Emily "committed" this poem to future genera-tions, she had no way of foreseeing that in the twentieth century it would be transformed into a famous modern dance, "Letter to the World." Martha Graham augmented her choreography with spoken words from Dickinson's poetry to tell the story of the strug-gles in the poet's interior life and to pay homage to her genius.

Another development that exceeded Dickinson's expectation is the international scope of the "World" she hoped to reach. The works of this stay-at-home New England poet, who never ventured outside her own country, are currently read in English throughout the world and have been translated into many languages, including Japanese, Czech, Polish, French, German, Italian, Danish, Dutch, Spanish, and Portuguese. The "World" that in this poem never wrote to her has become her universal correspondent.

23

Blotting Out the Light
I heard a Fly buzz when I died (1863)

I heard a Fly buzz – when I died –
The Stillness in the Room
Was like the Stillness in the Air –
Between the Heaves of Storm –

The Eyes around – had wrung them dry –
And Breaths were gathering firm
For that last Onset – when the King
Be witnessed – in the Room –

I willed my Keepsakes – Signed away
What portion of me be
Assignable – and then it was
There interposed a Fly –

With Blue – uncertain – stumbling Buzz –
Between the light – and me –
And then the Windows failed – and then
I could not see to see –

*E*mily was in her early twenties when she wrote to her friend Jane Humphrey about what it might be like to be dead and laid out for burial:

Bye and bye we'll be all gone, Jennie, does it
seem as if we would? The other day I tried to
think how I should look with my eyes shut,
and a little white gown on, and a snow-drop
on my breast; and I fancied I heard the
neighbors stealing in so softly to look down
in my face – so fast asleep – so still – Oh
Jennie, will you and I really become like this?

A Trauma Re-imagined

This imaginary scene of herself as a corpse bears a close
resemblance to the death-watch she had experienced when she
was thirteen years old at the bedside of her teenaged friend
Sophia Holland, who lay dying of typhoid fever. She remembers
that she "stole softly" in and looked down at her face, much as
she imagines, eight years later in her letter, "neighbors stealing
in so softly to look down in my face" as she lies dead. Devastating
as she finds the thought of death, the image she projects of her
dead body laid out for viewing – with "a little white gown on and
a snow-drop on my breast" – is mild and sentimental, perhaps in
deference to her correspondent's sensibilities. (In the letter she
adds, "Don't mind what I say, Darling, I'm a naughty, bad girl to
say sad things and make you cry") Nevertheless, the final thought
– "Oh Jennie, will you and I really become like this?" – remains
a disturbing question.

Writing the Poem

No such constraints to keep "sad things" at bay were hold-
ing her back when she wrote this poem in 1863. She was thirty-
three years old and in her poetic prime. The poem was not
intended for anyone but herself – except perhaps ultimately for
posterity – and she was free to envision as grim a scenario as she
chose. The setting, the situation – and the stillness – are the same
in the poem as in her letter to Jane Humphrey, but otherwise

the experience described by the speaker in the poem is very different from the one Emily imagined in Jane's letter. In the poem, the speaker is not yet a corpse. Far from being "fast asleep," her mind is racing with concerns about what she will leave behind and when death will arrive. Instead of her eyes being shut, she is struggling to the very end to "see." But the truly jarring addition is the stumbling buzz of a persistent fly.

The Deathbed Rituals of Her Day

With the ever-present specter of death a given in Emily's world, she would have known about the traditions surrounding the death of a family member at home. The custom usually "began with last minute bequests" in the presence of family and friends, followed by "the dying one giving witness in words to the Redeemer's presence in the room" before the final "grand act of passing." Dickinson's poem incorporates many of these standard features. There is the signing away of keepsakes and the expectation of the arrival of Christ ("that last Onset – when the King / Be witnessed – in the Room"), but just when there should have been a glorious welcoming of the light of heaven, a common household fly blocks out light altogether.

As Charles Anderson observes, Dickinson's poem "operates in terms of all the standard religious assumptions of her New England" but then turns the "meaning against itself," creating an ironic reversal. The "only sound of heavenly music or of wings taking flight" that fills the persona's dying ear is the "uncertain stumbling buzz of a fly." The poem's great irony, according to another reader, is that at the moment of death no "King" is witnessed – only a fly. The most bitter reading of the poem is Vivian Pollak's. In her view, the poem is a dark satire wherein fraud is not merely the essence of life; it is the essence of death as well. A letter Emily wrote in 1856 to her friend John Graves supports these ironic interpretations:

> To live and die, and mount again in tri-
> umphant body, and next time, try the upper
> air – is no schoolboy's theme! It is a jolly
> thought to think we can be Eternal – when
> air and earth are full of lives that are gone –
> and done – and a conceited thing indeed,
> this promised Resurrection.

The "promised Resurrection" was central to the deathbed ritual she mimics in the poem. But she calls the idea that "we can be Eternal . . . a conceited thing" foolish and egotistical in the face of the evidence of the dead who are no longer with us. These are serious matters, no longer themes a schoolboy might toy with. This passage is a surprisingly candid statement in a letter that foreshadows the skeptical outlook in the poem.

Imagery from a Sermon

An intense emotional experience that Emily had in church ten years before she wrote this poem may have provided her with some of its imagery. In a letter to her brother, she describes the sermon's effect on her:

> We had such a splendid sermon . . . I never
> heard anything like it, and don't expect to
> again, till we stand at the great white throne
> . . . it [the church] was very full, and still – so
> still, the buzzing of a fly would have boomed
> like a cannon. And when it was all over, and
> that wonderful man sat down, people stared
> at each other, and looked as wan and wild,
> as if they had seen a spirit and wondered
> they had not died.

Three concepts in this letter will surface in a new guise a decade later in this poem: the reference to standing "at the great white throne" (in the presence of God when life is over); the congregation's awed reaction as if they had been in the presence of death; and the profound stillness in which "the buzzing of a fly" would have broken the silence.

The Fly, Its Sources and Significance

Several other sources for the fly have been suggested. Emily may have been echoing, consciously or not, one of her favorite authors, Elizabeth Barrett Browning. In Book VI of *Aurora Leigh*, a poem Emily admired, Browning uses imagery involving a buzzing fly, as well as a dimming light.

Or Emily may have been drawing on her knowledge of the Bible, one of her favorite books. She would have known that in the Bible, Beelzebub, one of Satan's demons, is called the Lord of the Flies. If the fly is seen as representative of the devil, the darkness that ensues when it interposes between the light and the speaker is the permanent darkness of the spirit in Hell. Such an interpretation has led one reader to identify the fictional speaker in the poem as a soul already in Hell, recalling her dying moments.

A more mundane origin for the fly is Emily's own exposure to flies when she occasionally helped with the kitchen chores at the Homestead. She would know from her own observations that flies take on a bluish hue, stumble in their flight, and are persistent, just as they appear in the poem: "with Blue – uncertain – stumbling Buzz." Like any housewife, she would have abhorred houseflies: they pollute everything they touch, their eggs become maggots, and – like buzzards – they feed on carrion. They are associated with "putrefaction," and in one gruesome reading, the fly's buzz suggests "the fly's anticipation of her as decaying flesh."

What Goes First, Seeing or Hearing?

When the poet delineates what she imagines it might be like to die, she envisions hearing as the last sense to go. The nuances of the verb tenses in the poem somewhat blur the actual moment of death, but a close reading confirms that the dying speaker can still hear after she can no longer see. Everything between the first line, "I heard a fly buzz when I died," and the last line, "I could not see to see," is told as a flashback, so that the buzzing of the fly from the first line is concurrent with her loss of sight in the last line. At the end, she cannot see, but she can still hear the buzzing of the fly.

This idea – that our final remaining sense is hearing – continued to preoccupy Emily long after she had written this poem. In a letter she wrote in 1874, she observed: "The Ear is the last Face [of Death]. We hear after we see. Which to tell you first is still my Dismay." Twelve years earlier, she had skillfully used aural and visual imagery to effectively convey her "Dismay."

What It Means to "See"

In any meaningful attempt to interpret this poem, the issue that must be addressed is the double use of "see" in the last line: "I could not see to see." Two meanings for "see" are possible: (1) physical sight and (2) the ability to know, as in "I see what you mean." At the end of the poem, the persona confronts two losses: she has lost her eyesight, but she has also lost the mental ability to think, to know, to understand. The ultimate horror of death would be to lose the consciousness of one's very self.

One of Dickinson's strongest convictions was that consciousness was an indispensable part of being human, a precious commodity that guaranteed awareness of what one thinks and feels. In one letter, she likens it to an ennobling gladness; in another, she writes: "Consciousness is the only home of which we now know." Her emphasis on "now" implies that in the future there may not be a place where our knowledge can be housed – and then we "could not see to see."

This concern about consciousness surfaces repeatedly in

her poetry and in her letters, nowhere more vividly than when she expresses the enormity of its loss in the final line of this alarming and audacious poem.

24

Weighing the Brain

The Brain is wider than the Sky (1863)

The Brain – is wider than the Sky –
For – put them side by side –
The one the other will contain
With ease – and You – beside –

The Brain is deeper than the sea –
For – hold them – Blue to Blue –
The one the other will absorb –
As Sponges – Buckets – do –

The Brain is just the weight of God –
For – Heft them – Pound for Pound –
And they will differ – if they do –
As Syllable from Sound –

*L*avinia Dickinson once attempted to describe her sister Emily's primary function in life – and it was not writing poetry. Instead, Lavinia said, "She had to think – she was the only one of us who had that to do." She followed that tribute to her sister's formidable intellect with a comment that provides an insightful look at the dynamics of the Dickinson family. She added: "Father believed; and mother loved; and Austin had Amherst; and I had the family to keep track of." The family, each occupied in his or her own distinct way, appreciated Emily's unique gifts and together successfully created a haven for her where she could pursue her passion. None of them knew during all of Emily's lifetime that her "thinking" would result in a total of 1,789 poems, heralded today as the work of a genius.

One of these poems, "The Brain – is wider than the Sky," addresses the issue of thinking directly. It shows Emily using her thinking ability to write a poem about thinking. The brain is the stated subject, but it was consciousness that she was thinking about when she wrote this poem.

Thinking About Knowing

Emily's ideas about consciousness parallel what philosophers call epistemology, an age-old concept that has engaged thinkers as diverse as Descartes, Locke, and Kant. No evidence exists that Emily had any direct knowledge of these thinkers. A review of the curriculum at the schools Dickinson attended – Amherst Academy and Mount Holyoke Female Seminary – reveals no courses dealing with their ideas, nor does her reading encompass their works. Nevertheless, as this poem makes clear, Emily grappled with the same issues that these seventeenth- and eighteenth-century philosophers did. The basic question was – and still is – how do we know what we know?

The Infinity of the Brain

That question is at the heart of this poem. The speaker chooses to look for an answer by looking at the brain, the engine and the repository of human knowledge. She observes that it encompasses the entire external world, wider than the sky, and deeper than the ocean. When it comes to God, in the third and final stanza, the brain and God appear to be indistinguishable, the mind's supremacy striking an "easy equivalency" with God, "Pound for Pound."

According to one interpretation, the persona of this poem believes that nothing exists outside of "The Brain" – not even the "You" to whom the poem is addressed. Another reader suggests that Dickinson created a speaker who could stand "watchfully by her subjective self in order to examine" how her consciousness works.

The Idea of God

This is one of the many poems that Dickinson never shared with anyone. She was surely aware that her contemporaries would have been shocked at its implication that God might be a creation of the human mind or, as one reader put it, that God is "neither more nor less than what we are capable of imagining."

But, as is often the case with a Dickinson poem, before a definite conclusion can be reached, the reader is presented with a caveat, a warning. In the last two lines, we are told that consciousness and God may differ after all, and if they do, it's the way "Syllable" differs from "Sound." The meaning of that enigmatic distinction has been variously interpreted. Robert Wiesbuch, for example, asserts that the difference is "between the thing itself and its imperfect, itemized explanation." David Porter sees the distinction between the mortal brain and God as being that "God works through silent revelation, whereas the poet reveals through language." According to Helen Vendler, the poet reframes "in intelligible Syllables the unintelligible Sounds ascribable to God," thereby leading to the sacrilegious conclusion that the human brain is superior to God.

A Thoroughly Modern Poet

Dickinson does not provide us with foolproof answers. She merely expresses her thought processes through poetry. Her fascination with human consciousness, and her fearless exploration of it, make her writing strikingly modern. They align her with scholars and scientists in the twenty-first century who work with the same issues. At the University of Pennsylvania, experts from the fields of medicine, pastoral care, religious studies, social work, and bioethics have created a new Center for Spirituality and the Mind. They use brain-imaging technology to attempt to answer such questions as "Does God exist outside the human mind, or is God a creation of our brains?" A leading behavioral neurologist, Antonio Damasio, has developed a new framework under which to examine consciousness that takes into account the physiology of the brain and the psychology of the emotions.

Almost 150 years ago, using nothing but her brain – and the intelligence and imagination it contained – Emily Dickinson pursued answers to the same questions. Her poetry, as relevant as ever, continues to confront its readers with these universal dilemmas. It succeeds in making thinkers of us all.

25

The Insane Majority

Much Madness is divinest Sense (1863)

Much Madness is divinest Sense –
To a discerning Eye –
Much Sense – the starkest Madness –
'Tis the Majority
In this, as all, prevail –
Assent – and you are sane –
Demur – you're straightway dangerous –
And handled with a Chain –

*E*mily recognized, early on, that she was different from most of the people in her social world. She learned from experience that much of the difference had to do with her mental state and her attitude toward the "majority," who set the standard for what was normal. She wrote a letter in 1861 that included a candid admission about just how different she was – and how her world reacted to such deviations from the established norm. The key passage makes the following observation: "Think Emily lost her wits – but she found 'em, likely. Don't part with wits long at a time in this neighborhood."

A Deliberately Circuitous Statement

At first glance, she appears to be treating the incident light-heartedly. But she may simply have been following the advice she offers in another poem, "Tell all the truth but tell it slant," where she maintains that "Success in Circuit lies." The casual tone masks a deadly serious subject.

The circuitousness begins with her decision to speak of herself in the third person, a device that allows for a meaningful ambiguity. Who is it that thinks Emily has lost her wits? She doesn't provide the noun or pronoun that goes with the verb. Is it "I" (the speaker who thinks "Emily lost her wits") or is it "they" – the "neighborhood"?

The most ambiguous word, however, is "likely," as used in "but she found 'em, likely." It could mean "perhaps" in the sense that it is only "likely" that she recovered and she may still be mentally unbalanced, OR that she didn't recover her wits because she didn't need to. She had never lost them to begin with. In light of the sentence that follows, "likely" takes on a different significance. It could mean she had been acting "like" ("as if") she had found her wits in order to conform to the neighborhood's concept of sane behavior. The implication in that last sentence is that the consequences for her would be dire enough to be unacceptable, and that she had to try to stop being different.

Letter and Poem Aligned

Two years after that letter, she wrote "Much madness is divinest Sense," a poem that gives a more straightforward account of what happens when your neighbors decide you have lost your wits in a neighborhood where no one is allowed to be different for long. The parallels between this poem and the letter quoted above are striking. In both, the powerful majority – the neighborhood – prevails. Did Emily do what her poem says is necessary to appease the Majority? Did she "Assent" to their requirements? We cannot know for sure, but her poetry and her letters reveal that she did learn to adapt. We know she learned to tell the truth "slant" and that she showed great restraint in sharing her more shocking poems with others. We know she gradually retreated from the outside world, limiting her contact with the "neighborhood," where she might have been seen as too different.

Chaining the Lunatics

As early as 1852, nine years before the confrontation with her "neighborhood," she actually thought about the possibility of ending up in chains in an insane asylum. She wrote, "in thinking of those I love, my reason is all gone from me, and I do fear sometimes that I must make a hospital for the hopelessly insane, and chain me up there such times." That thought reappears in this poem's startling final image – the lunatic "handled with a Chain."

Whatever Emily knew about the "hopelessly insane" being put in chains could well have come through her father, who had a lifelong interest in insane asylums. In college, Edward Dickinson wrote an essay titled "The importance of providing an Asylum for the insane." Later in life, he was a staunch supporter of the Worcester Hospital for the Insane and served as a trustee of the State Lunatic Hospital at Northampton. When Emily was thirteen and away from home on a month-long recuperative visit, her father's concern for her included some unusual advice. He wrote, "I want to have you see the Lunatic Hospital, & other interesting places in Worcester." His recommendation is all the more surprising when we consider that Emily was recuperating from depression following the death of a beloved girlfriend. We don't know whether she ever followed her father's suggestion and actually saw asylum inmates in chains, or whether her troubled imagination was at work again.

A Troubled Time

Emily's unsettled mental state was on her mind in several of her letters and poems in the years between 1861 and 1863. She wrote to Higginson about a "terror" she experienced in 1861, the same year of the "neighborhood" letter to her cousins. She provided no details, but one of the possibilities that have been proposed is that she suffered a terrifying mental breakdown. In 1862, she wrote "I felt a Funeral in my Brain," a poem that describes what it is like when "a plank in reason, broke." John Cody, medical doctor turned literary biographer, cites it as revealing the "height of turmoil and psychic disintegration." In an 1863 letter she admits she feels "a snarl in the brain which don't unravel yet," a phenomenon that reappears in a poem she wrote the next year, "I felt a Cleaving in my Mind." The metaphor is different – a split in the brain that she cannot fit back together, rather than a snarl in the brain that she cannot unravel – but both describe a profound mental disturbance. She was aware that she sometimes acted irrationally and was concerned about it.

Recognizing Emily's "Wildness"

Emily could not have had any tangible proof that two of the people closest to her shared her concern about her mental instability, but as sensitive and intuitive as she was, she must have been aware of it at some level. The two were Austin, her brother, and Thomas Higginson, her mentor.

"She is rather too wild at present" was Austin's explanation as to why a family friend would not be hearing from Emily. Austin and Emily had received duplicate letters urging them to publicly accept Christ as their personal savior. Austin added that he presumed Emily "will not answer" and asked that Emily not be contacted again. Apparently, Austin had no compunctions about characterizing his nineteen-year old-sister as "too wild" – and all that it suggests: out of control, unbalanced, and unrestrained.

Higginson too expressed doubt as to Emily's mental stability. He described her on one occasion as "my partially cracked poetess at Amherst." Whatever else he may have told his wife about Emily, Mrs. Higginson is reputed to have exclaimed, "Oh why do the insane so cling to you?"

The "Divine Insanity" of Poetry

In 1863, shortly before she wrote "Much madness," Dickinson wrote a poem that presents madness from a different perspective – as the source of divine inspiration for the writing of poetry. The poem "I think I was enchanted" was written as a tribute to Elizabeth Barrett Browning, shortly after the news of Browning's death reached her. Dickinson's poem glories in the "Lunacy" the speaker experienced upon first reading Browning's poetry. The poem goes on to warn that "The Danger [is] to be sane," prefiguring the third line of "Much madness," where "Much Sense" is "the starkest Madness." "'Twas a Divine Insanity," the poet declares further along in her eulogy to Browning, summing up and defending her view of what it takes to write poetry.

Coping with the Insane Majority

Years before she wrote "Much Madness," where she opposes the right of the majority to be the arbiter of madness, she expressed similar ideas in letters to two of her friends. In 1856, she wrote, "Pardon my sanity, Mrs. Holland, in a world insane." In 1859, she wrote to Kate Scott, "Insanity to the sane seems so unnecessary – but I am only one, and they are 'four and forty,' which little affair of numbers leaves me impotent." Both statements foreshadow the conclusions she comes to in the poem: that the majority are often insane; that the speaker places herself among the supposedly insane minority who have "a discerning eye" (enabling them to see reality clearly); and that "the numbers" have the power to render her (the "only one" dissenting) helpless.

A Long Lasting Resonance

"Much madness" is an immensely quotable poem. It lends itself to many situations in which the majority appear to have taken an irrational stand in the opinion of a discerning minority.

Emily Dickinson may have been a minority of one in Amherst in her day, but since then her poem has resonated with a multitude of readers. Like her, they find themselves at odds with the majority who prevail.

26

An Out-of-Body Seaside Walk
I started Early – Took my Dog (1863)

I started Early – Took my Dog –
And visited the Sea –
The Mermaids in the Basement
Came out to look at me –

And Frigates – in the Upper Floor
Extended Hempen Hands –
Presuming Me to be a Mouse –
Aground – opon the Sands –

But no Man moved Me – till the Tide
Went past my simple Shoe –
And past my Apron – and my Belt
And past my Boddice – too –

And made as He would eat me up –
As wholly as a Dew
Opon a Dandelion's Sleeve –
And then – I started – too –

And He – He followed – close behind –
I felt His Silver Heel
Opon my ancle – Then My Shoes
Would overflow with Pearl –

Until We met the Solid Town –
No One He seemed to know –
And bowing – with a Mighty look –
At me – The Sea withdrew –

The biographical connections in this poem are highly tentative at best. No evidence exists that Emily ever took a walk along the seashore, with or without a dog. She may have seen the sea when she was thirteen during a visit in Boston with her Aunt Lavinia Norcross, or on a subsequent visit to Boston two years later, but there is no reference to any such experience in the surviving letters. In fact, when she wrote this poem in 1863, Emily had spent most of her life at home in Amherst. The few other times she had been away were in equally land-locked places: a year at school at Mount Holyoke; two visits with family friends, the Hollands, in Springfield, Massachusetts; a trip to Washington and Philadelphia while her father was a member of Congress; and her last social visit away from Amherst to Middletown, Connecticut, in 1860. When the speaker in another poem claims "I never saw the sea," she bears a close resemblance to the poet herself.

Not a "Real" Sea

One Dickinson scholar, Robert Weisbuch, states his position on this issue bluntly: the sea in this poem "has absolutely nothing in common with any body of water anyone has ever visited." The "Mermaids" in the opening verse are a dead giveaway; the scene is not a literal one and has no identifiable geographical location. Rather, it is another testament to Dickinson's faith in her fertile imagination, the same conviction she attests to in "I never saw a Moor" (written a year later.) Jack Capps, who has done an in-depth study of Emily's reading, proposes that the poem's opening lines reflect a seaside description in one of her textbooks.

A Very Real Dog

The dog, however, is real – and Emily did take him for walks. When asked about her companions, she counted chief among them "a Dog – large as myself, that my father bought me." She named him Carlo after the dog in a favorite book of hers, Ik Marvell's *Reveries of a Bachelor*. Carlo was a part of her daily life for more than fifteen years, and he appears in over forty of her letters and poems. A friend recalls taking a walk with Emily "while the huge dog stalked solemnly beside them." Emily turned to her young friend and said, "Gracie . . . do you know that I believe that the first to come and greet me when I go to heaven will be this dear, faithful old friend Carlo." In one letter, she refers to "my Carlo," adding "The Dog is the noblest work of Art." Given her feelings for her dog, he seems a natural choice to accompany her on this imaginative encounter with the sea.

The Sea as Symbol

What the sea represents is key to the poem's meaning. A few early interpretations viewed the sea as "the traditional symbol of death." More and more readers, however, have come to believe that the sea symbolizes sexual love, as it does in such love poems as "Wild nights – Wild nights!" and "Come slowly – Eden," but with a crucial difference: the love poems are totally consensual, while the speaker's role in this poem is ambivalent.

Readers' interpretations have varied widely. At one extreme, Carrie O'Maley finds the poet depicting "a first enjoyable sexual encounter," while William Shurr claims a middle ground. He deems the speaker to be a "not entirely unwilling damsel." At the other end of the spectrum, Shawn Alfrey claims that the poem reflects the "erotics of heterosexual rape." The poem has been called "a sexual nightmare" and "a study in fear [and] abject terror." The poem's strength lies in the fact that it can accommodate these contradictory interpretations and still remain "superbly dramatic and highly symbolic."

Psychological Perspectives

A psychoanalytic perspective is offered by John Cody, a psychiatrist who immersed himself in the study of Dickinson's poetry and letters. He believes that the sea in this poem represents "the vast unconscious." Drowning in it depicts "the loss of one's psychic integrity." The persona "becomes aware of the possibility of imminent drowning – inundation by the unconscious and the instinctual drives, especially the erotic ones. The ego defenses are at last heeded and the speaker beats a panicky retreat from the unconscious. She returns to reality, 'the Solid Town' so unlike the fluid fantasies of the id."

Eric Carlson covers the same psychological terrain in lay terms: the poem is a "dramatization of the frightening realization that toying with love may arouse a tide of emotion too powerful to control."

An Overview and Conclusions

In response to what she calls the poem's invitation to extravagant interpretation, Joan Kirkby obliges with a comprehensive overview. The poem is about an encounter between nature (the sea) and culture (the town.) The domesticated dog is an intermediary between the two. It is also about an encounter between the conscious mind (the boats in the upper storey) and the unconscious (the mermaids in the basement.) The sea becomes a would-be molester, suggesting an unleashing of repressed sexual energy that now threatens to overwhelm the speaker.

Fictional as this persona and her seaside adventure may be on a literal level, Emily confronted the same threat as that facing the poem's protagonist: the loss of her self-identity. Emily fought all her life against great odds to be what she wanted most to be

– a poet. One of the distractions that would have prevented her from reaching that goal was sexual fulfillment, something that was available to her only through marriage. She may have been tempted temporarily, but as this poem – and her entire canon – confirm, she successfully averted the dangers that threatened her identity. She stayed true to herself.

Saying No to Life
I cannot live with You (1863)

I cannot live with You –
It would be Life –
And Life is over there –
Behind the Shelf

The Sexton keeps the key to –
Putting up
Our life – His Porcelain –
Like a Cup –

Discarded of the Housewife –
Quaint – or Broke –
A newer Sevres pleases –
Old Ones crack –

I could not die – with You –
For one must wait
To shut the Other's Gaze down –
You – could not -

And I – Could I stand by
And see You – freeze –
Without my Right of Frost –
Death's privilege?

Nor could I rise – with You –
Because your Face
Would put out Jesus' –
That New Grace

Grown plain – and foreign
On my homesick eye –
Except that You than He
Shone closer by –

They'd judge Us – How –
For You – served Heaven – You know
Or sought to –
I could not –

Because You saturated sight –
And I had no more eyes
For sordid excellence
As Paradise

And were You lost, I would be –
Though my name
Rang loudest
On the Heavenly fame –

And were You – saved –
And I – condemned to be
Where You were not
That self – were hell to me –

So we must meet apart –
You there – I – here –
With just the Door ajar
That Oceans are – and Prayer –
And that White Sustenance –
Despair –

$\mathcal{B}$etween 1858 and 1861, Emily wrote three love letters in draft form to a mysterious "Master" whom she never identified. The strongest contender for that role is the Reverend Charles Wadsworth. He is also, in all probability, the man being addressed in this poem, the "You" with whom the persona "cannot live."

Emily met Wadsworth in Philadelphia in 1855. He visited her at the Homestead in 1860, after she had initiated a correspondence asking for his spiritual guidance. The erotic poems she wrote in 1861, "Wild nights – Wild nights!" and "Come slowly – Eden!", are often associated with the "Master" of the draft letters, but evidence of the Wadsworth connection is circumstantial at best.

By 1863, when Emily wrote this poem, whether this romance was a fantasy of hers or based on mutual attraction, enough time had elapsed that the impossibility of any kind of long-term relationship would have been clear. What this poem provides is a set of striking similarities between the "You" in the poem and Wadsworth, as well as between the persona and Emily. Like the "You" in the poem, Wadsworth, a Presbyterian minister "served Heaven." He was married, and line 29 ("They'd judge us") suggests the moral condemnation they would be subjected to if their adulterous love were consummated. Equally damning would be the persona's unorthodox Christianity, paralleling

Emily's own attitude toward church dogma. This is expressed in the sacrilegious sixth verse: "Nor could I rise – with You – / Because Your Face / Would put out Jesus'."

Also like the lover (in line 48 of the poem) Wadsworth was literally "Oceans" away when Emily wrote this poem. He had accepted a post in San Francisco the previous year and had sailed there over two oceans, the Atlantic and the Pacific, by way of the Isthmus of Panama.

Renunciation in Poetry and in Life

Whoever the original impetus for this poem may have been, the poetry tells us much more about the poet than about any lover she may or may not have had. Renunciation played a key role in Emily's life; in this poem it is at its very core.

Helen Vendler calls this a "heartbreaking poem" of "erotic deprivation." The narrative covers a series of losses: she gives up her beloved in life ("I cannot live with You"); she gives him up in death ("I could not die – with You); and she gives him up in life after death ("Nor could I rise with you"). Like Emily, the persona accepts the oxymoron that "We must meet apart," acknowledging that the future does not hold a life together for them.

Mixing the Sexual and the Divine

In keeping with the poem's pattern based on the tension between "Life" on earth and "Life" eternal, the poet mixes domestic metaphors with divine imagery: the sexton's chalice is like "a Cup – Discarded of the Housewife" (lines 8-9). The poem follows a narrative structure that moves through life, communion, death, and resurrection, deliberately conflating the sexual and the religious in the climactic word that ends the poem: "Despair."

A Long-Delayed Fulfillment

Eighteen years after she wrote this poem, Emily was forty-seven years old and once again writing passionate love letters.

However, these letters were not addressed to an illusory unidentifiable "Master" but to a flesh-and-blood man who returned her love. Otis Phillips Lord was sixty-eight, a Massachusetts Supreme Court judge who had been a close friend of her father's. Emily and Lord began writing to each other in 1881, just months after his wife died, and the letters continued, in between his visits to the Homestead, until his sudden death in 1884. Also, unlike the longing and angst of the "Master" letters, these express exuberant joy. Playfully addressing him in the third person, she describes her feelings this way: "I confess that I love him – I rejoice that I love him – I thank the maker of Heaven and Earth – that gave him me to love – the exultation floods me. I cannot find my channel – the Creek turns Sea – at thought of thee."

Emily uses sea imagery here ("floods," "channel," "Creek," "Sea") to evoke erotic abandonment as she did in "Wild nights," written two decades earlier during the time of the "Master" letters. A possible answer to whether Emily's affair with Judge Lord was as physically sensual as the one Emily describes in her "Wild nights" poem comes from a surprising source: her sister-in-law. Sue told a friend that she had gone next door to the Homestead one day, and in the drawing room "found Emily reclining in the arms of a man." Sue had her own reason for portraying Emily in such scandalous terms; she was angry with what she considered Lavinia and Emily's approval of her husband's affair with Mabel Todd. Whatever Sue's motivation may have been, Emily's letters to Lord do indeed attest to her sexual passion. She writes: "I do – do want you tenderly. The air is soft as Italy, but when it touches me, I spurn it with a Sigh, because it is not you." She also writes: "Don't you know you are happiest while I withhold and not confer – don't you know that No is the wildest word we consign to Language? . . . I will not let you cross – but it is all your's, and when it is right I will lift the Bars, and lay you in the Moss." Whether she ever did "lift the Bars" is unknown.

No Married Happily Ever After

We do know, however, that Emily never did marry Judge Lord. The "Life" that in the opening verse of "I cannot live with You" is consigned to "over there / Behind the shelf," had finally became accessible to her, but that dream never became a reality. The reasons are complex and unclear. Judge Lord's niece, who would have been his primary heir, objected to it. Both Lord and Emily were beset with illnesses in the 1880s, and since he wanted to take her away to live with him in Salem, she may have been unable to overcome the agoraphobic tendencies that had kept her at home for decades. Nevertheless, for those three years before Lord's death, Emily knew what it was like to love a man she knew loved her. At her funeral her sister, Vinnie, put two heliotropes in her casket "by her hand 'to take to Judge Lord.'"

28

Taking It on Faith

I never saw a Moor (1864)

I never saw a Moor.
I never saw the Sea –
Yet know I how the Heather looks.
And what a Billow be –

I never spoke with God,
Nor visited in heaven –
Yet certain am I of the spot
As if the chart were given –

*T*he upbeat, affirming message combined with the accessible, informal language of this poem has made it one of Dickinson's most popular poems. It is often quoted as proof positive of her faith in God and Heaven, but nothing is ever quite what it seems in the writings of this most ambivalent of poets.

Letters Filled with Doubts

A review of her life up to 1864, when she wrote this poem, reveals some decidedly anti-God tendencies. When she was sixteen years old and a student at Amherst Academy, she was under intense pressure to respond to the religious revivals being held on campus. She confided her conflicted feelings to her friend Abiah Root: "I am continually putting off becoming a

Christian." When she left Amherst Academy, she was one of a small minority at the school who had resisted conversion. Four years later in 1850, back home at the Homestead, in the midst of another wave of revivals in Amherst, she wrote to another friend, "Christ is calling everyone here . . . I am standing alone in rebellion." That year her father, her sister, and her best friend, Susan Gilbert, accepted Christ as their personal savior. Emily, however, persisted – in her own quiet way – in her "rebellion": she never did join the church and eventually stopped attending the services altogether.

She continued to express her views candidly in her letters. Her disdain for the traditional concept of God is especially clear in what appears to be a response to a question asked by Thomas Higginson about her family. She wrote, "They are religious – except me – and address an Eclipse, every morning – whom they call their 'Father.'" The sacrilege takes a different form in another letter in which she looks back at her early enthusiastic response to "the Lord Jesus Christ" and admits she could have easily believed in Santa Claus in the same way. As for her belief in a heaven after death, she dismisses the "promised Resurrection" as merely a "conceited thing" in the light of all those whose deaths she has witnessed.

Blasphemy in the Poems Too

Some representative samples of the poems she wrote before this one are just as blasphemous. In "I never lost as much but twice" she calls God a "Burglar." In another, she declares "Faith is a fine invention" and advocates science as a more prudent option. And in "The brain is wider than the sky" she implies that God may be merely a creation of the human mind. With such a history, what is the reader to make of the belief in God expressed in this poem? Perhaps it should be read as a conundrum for the poet as much as for the reader.

Sure of Her Belief in Nature

A passage in a letter Emily wrote to her friend Mrs. Holland, two years or so after she wrote this poem, sheds some light on what the poet meant in this so-called declaration of faith. The letter touches on the same issues raised in the poem:

> I saw the sunrise on the Alps since I saw
> you. Travel why to Nature, when she dwells
> with us? Those who lift their hats shall see
> her, as [the] devout do God.

In this passage, Emily claims she "saw" the sunrise on the Alps, although she has never physically been there. Similarly, in this poem the speaker says she "knows" what the moor and the sea look like without having literally "seen" them. The sunrise in the Alps, the moor, and the sea are all aspects of Nature that, according to the letter, "dwells with us" and can be seen by "those" who are willing to look up ("Those who lift their hats.") Emily had never traveled outside the United States and had never been to the Alps. Her point was that she didn't have to go there to see them. She could imagine their beauty (perhaps aided by her adventures in reading) and make it real for herself. Her faith in the imagination as expressed in the images of nature in the first verse is something that the poet herself could easily accept.

Not So Sure of Her Belief in God

The faith evoked in the second verse is a different matter. Where Emily, who wrote the letter, differs from the persona, who speaks in the poem, is that when she wrote this poem, she was rebelling against her religion and its God. In the letter to Mrs. Holland quoted above, she merely points out the similarity between her faith in Nature and the faith of the "devout" in God. The biographical evidence suggests that at this point in her life she does not consider herself one of the "devout."

Ironic or a Change of Heart?

The question of how to read the poem centers on this basic issue of her faith in God and her belief in the immortality promised by Christianity. Given the facts of her life, the poem appears to be ironic. Several readers have interpreted it as such. Robert Merideth reads it as a "critique of the values of her time." Clark Griffith believes it would be a distortion to make this poem Dickinson's "trademark," claiming that at best it could be thought of as "whistling in the dark."

However, many take the poem at its face value. She may well have had a change of heart. George Monteiro sees it as "one of Dickinson's clearest declarations of spiritual calm and religious faith." For Robert Lair, it conveys the poet's "childlike faith in God." Cynthia Woolf hears in it an echo of the popular nineteenth-century "consolation" literature that Emily enjoyed reading. She believes that Dickinson's best poetry denounces God but that the dynamic of hope and despair was constantly at work in her. Here Emily was expressing her hopes.

Richard Sewall explains her inconsistencies as records of the stages of a pilgrimage. He calls her "an experimenter of the spirit," each contradiction another setback in the faith she kept seeking.

Following the Metrics of Watts's Hymns

As in much of her poetry, Dickinson's form in this poem follows the metrics used by Isaac Watts, whose hymns she heard in the church services she attended while she was growing up. She adapts Watts's short meter (two six-syllable lines, followed by one of eight syllables, then one of six syllables – 6/6/8/6) as well as his customary rhyme scheme (abab – but with one near rhyme). What's more, the second stanza is identical in subject matter to a stanza in one of Watts's hymns, but with significant differences in the relationship of the speaker to God. Again the question arises as to whether Dickinson's poem is a parody of Watts or more of a counterpoint.

Readers may disagree about whether or not the poem affirms her faith in God, but there is little doubt that it affirms her faith in the imagination. Her imagination was what Robert Frost admired when he called her "the best of all women poets who ever wrote." He claimed that the power of her poetry, fueled as it was by her imagination, proved that poets need not go to Niagara to write about the force of falling water.

29

The Poet as a Boy
A narrow Fellow in the Grass (1865)

A narrow Fellow in the Grass
Occasionally rides –
You may have met him? Did you not
His Notice instant is –

The Grass divides as with a Comb –
A spotted Shaft is seen,
And then it closes at your Feet
And opens further on –

He likes a Boggy Acre –
A Floor too cool for Corn –
But when a Boy and Barefoot
I more than once at morn

Have passed I thought a Whip Lash
Unbraiding in the sun
When stooping to secure it
It wrinkled And was gone –

Several of Nature's People
I know and they know me
I feel for them a transport
Of Cordiality

But never met this Fellow
Attended or alone
Without a tighter Breathing
And Zero at the Bone.

When Emily was "a little girl," her encounters with nature's creatures – including snakes – were primarily positive experiences. When she was a woman in her thirties, she remembered them this way:

> When much in the Woods as a little girl, I
> was told that the Snake would bite me, that I
> might pick a poisonous flower, or Goblins
> kidnap me, but I went along and met no one
> but Angels, who were far more shyer of me,
> than I could be of them, so I havn't that con-
> fidence in fraud which many exercise.

About a decade earlier, however, she appears to have thought differently about them, at least about snakes. She is in a light-hearted, teasing mood when she refers to snakes in a letter to her friend Abiah Root. She admonishes her not to be taken in by some of the things she writes in her letters. They are "fictions," she says, "vain imaginations to lead astray foolish young women." They "tell deliberate falsehoods, avoid them as the snake," she cautions. Then she continues on a more somber note: "Honestly, tho', a snake bite is a serious matter . . . 'Verily I say unto you fear him.'" Her ambivalence about this "narrow fellow in the grass" emerges again when she adds, "I love those little green ones that slide around by your shoes in the grass –

and make it rustle with their elbows – they are rather my favorites on the whole."

Emily may still have been having a bit of fun when she chose a snake as a subject for one of the 229 poems she wrote in 1865. If so, the joke is at the reader's expense, because the cordiality expressed toward nature in the first five verses of "A narrow Fellow in the Grass" comes to an abrupt halt with a jolting reversal in the sixth and final verse. The last line of this poem is one of Dickinson's most famous – and most effective – tactile images. "Zero at the bone" resonates viscerally, while the "tighter Breathing" that immediately precedes it enhances the chest-tightening, bone-chilling effect.

The opening description of the snake fits those "little green ones that slide around by your shoes in the grass" that she earlier claimed she loved and called her favorites. The fifth verse presents a cozy picture of close intimacy with "nature's people" – only to lead to a finale fraught with fear and a climax filled with an icy realization of danger.

Sights and Sounds

In addition to the celebrated tactile imagery in the poem's final lines, visual and auditory elements have also been singled out for praise. One example is the remarkable exactness with which the snake's movements have been captured: first, he is seen momentarily as "A spotted shaft," then, in a combination of sight with movement, he is "a Whip Lash, Unbraiding." He is present even when invisible as he parts the grass and then opens it again at the speaker's feet. Sound enforces the reader's response in the last verse where the long "o" in "Fellow" and "Zero," and the rhyming "alone" and "bone," mimics the narrator's indrawn breath of shock and realization. The "s" sounds in the first verse – "His notice sudden is" – captures the hissing sound of the snake and announces its presence.

Biblical Echoes

Given Dickinson's "extraordinary" knowledge of the Bible, no snake-in-the-grass in her world is likely to be far removed from the snake in the Garden of Eden described in Genesis. Emily was raised in a Bible-reading family. Whenever her father was home, he began the day by reading from the Bible. According to one of her biographers, "She knew every line of the Bible intimately, quoted from it extensively, and referred to it many times more often than she referred to any other work."

Emily's snake references bear several striking similarities to the snake in Genesis, where he personifies the Devil. He is infamous for his lies, and in the letter to Abiah about snakes, she associates her own "deliberate falsehoods" with the snake's lies. Her "fictions" may "lead astray foolish young women" just as the snake in Genesis misled Eve.

Emily as a Boy

Readers are often taken aback when they get to the line "But when a Boy and Barefoot," but this is not the only time Emily assumes a male identity. She represents herself as a boy in eight other poems. In a note to her nephew Ned to accompany a gift of a pie, she refers to a time "when I was a Boy":

> You know that pie you stole – well, this is that
> Pie's brother. Mother told me when I was a
> Boy, that I must "turn over a new Leaf" – I
> call that the Foliage Admonition. Shall I com-
> mend it to you?

Aunt Emily is clearly joking with her nephew here – typical, according to Ned's sister Mattie, of the private jokes the two shared. In the same spirit, in an earlier letter Emily referred to herself as Ned's Uncle Emily.

Mattie and Ned's mother, Sue, also used the same wording in response to a question about a line in this poem. Sam Bowles, who was a mutual friend of Sue's and Emily's, asked, "How did that girl ever know that a boggy field wasn't good for corn?" Sue's reply was "Oh, you forget that was Emily 'when a boy'!"

Interpreting Her Sex Change

Emily's use of a male persona has elicited a variety of explanations. To one biographer, it was a way for her to look back at the "free and fearless outdoor sauntering as a defining activity of her life 'when a boy' – a phrase that became indispensable to her after her habits of seclusion were established."

Feminist readers see the situation differently. For them, Dickinson's assumption of a male role is associated with breaking down restrictive boundaries and trying to claim some of the dominant masculine power for her self. According to the poet Adrienne Rich, "Since the most powerful figures in patriarchal culture have been men, it seems natural that Dickinson would assign a masculine gender to that in herself which did not fit in with the conventional ideology of womanliness."

Robbed by a Friend

The publication history of this poem is unique: it is the only one that Emily claimed was "robbed" from her. It appeared on the front page of the *Springfield Republican* with the title "The Snake" on February 14, 1866. On March 17, Emily wrote to her mentor Higginson: "Lest you meet my Snake and suppose I deceive it was robbed of me . . . I had told you I did not print – I feared you might think me ostensible." Her sister-in-law, Sue, with whom Emily often shared her poetry, appears to have been the robber who gave the poem to their friend Sam Bowles, the editor of the *Springfield Republican*. Many years later, a woman who had grown up in Amherst remembered hearing Sue confess that its appearance in the newspaper "nearly caused a breach in the close friendship of the two."

A Sexual Subtext

Some readers have taken a psychosexual approach to their interpretations of this poem. For them, the snake is a phallic symbol, an expression of repressed sexuality, with the bare feet suggesting a sexual receptivity. The image of the snake as a "Whip Lash" is viewed as lending a sadomasochistic element to the dangerous encounter. Emily, who wrote explicitly erotic poetry when she chose to, would probably have rejected any such readings of this poem.

In keeping with the tradition of riddle poems that Dickinson enjoyed, she never uses the word "snake" in the poem, yet readers have no difficulty identifying its subject. One reader points out that the subject matter – an encounter with a snake – is not nearly as important as the effect of that meeting on the speaker. In turn, the reader – through Dickinson's genius with words – experiences the effect with her.

Dimming Truth's Dazzle

Tell all the truth but tell it slant (1872)

Tell all the truth but tell it slant –
Success in Circuit lies
Too bright for our infirm Delight
The Truth's superb surprise
As Lightning to the Children eased
With explanation kind
The Truth must dazzle gradually
Or every man be blind –

*I*n 1873, the year after Emily wrote this poem, her father arranged to have her examined on spiritual matters by the Reverend Jonathan Jenkins, minister of the First Church of Christ in Amherst. After the interrogation, he diagnosed her as theologically "sound." We don't know what questions and answers were exchanged during that interview, nor do we know of any specific incident that might have prompted Edward Dickinson to initiate such an investigation. Clearly he was worried about his daughter's psychological welfare. Emily was forty-two years old – and given her long-standing eccentricities, he may well have been troubled about her for quite a while.

As perceptive and astute as Emily was, she must have been aware of her father's concern. This poem offers some insight into what was on her mind the year before the Reverend Jenkins' examination. Taken in the context of her father's growing distress over her attitude toward Christianity, "Tell all the truth but tell it slant" can be interpreted as the advice she is giving to herself. She needs to express herself as indirectly as possible in order to cope with the negative fallout her ideas might generate. She must avoid drawing attention to her blasphemous pronunciations, whether in her letters or in her poetry – or even in her limited interaction with others.

She knew she still had to abide by the conventions demanded of her as a member of a prominent and publicly visible family if she expected that family to continue to support her. She had "a room of her own" and the opportunity to write poetry, the one thing in life she wanted most to do. If she expressed her radical beliefs openly and shocked her family and her community, she would jeopardize her situation. She needed to assuage her father's worries about her spiritual health. This poem reveals one ploy she could use to stay true to her principles while continuing to write.

In poetry, Dickinson had found an ideal vehicle for telling her slanted truth. Because it relies heavily on metaphor – saying one thing in terms of another – poetry is itself a slanted, roundabout means of expression. Dickinson expanded the metaphoric dimensions of poetry by extensive use of oxymorons, oblique descriptions, and familiar words in unusual contexts. The self-contradictory phrase "dazzle gradually" in the next-to-last line of the poem is a perfect example of her technique in action. Through "indirection and the unexpected," she reveals, in subtle ways, truths too shocking for her to declare outright.

Biblical Echoes and Religious Implications

A passage from the Bible has been proposed as a source for the imagery in the poem. Acts 9:4, wherein Paul is blinded by a great "light from Heaven," parallels the poet's assertion that such a direct confrontation with the "Truth" would be "Too bright" and leave us "blind."

In keeping with this religious source, one reader proposes that the "Truth's superb surprise" is God. He is the "omitted center" of the poem, not named specifically because it is not possible for mortal eyes to behold him or for mortal human beings to hear him speak to them directly.

An Unusual Publishing History

Emily scribbled this poem in pencil on a scrap of stationery in 1872. She never made a fair copy of it or included it in any of the fascicles in which she sometimes bound her poems. In fact, it was not "discovered" and published until 1945.

Since then, it has received a lot of attention as a poem that provides a key to understanding her poetry. New readers are sometimes put off by Dickinson's devious and circuitous techniques. It helps to know that often she deliberately tells the truth "slant." The roundabout journey we sometimes have to take to get to her "truth" is inevitably worth the effort.

The bonus that comes with this poem is the justification it gives to readers who may be faced with a similar dilemma – that is, wanting to be truthful but not wanting to cause havoc. Should we find ourselves faced with such a choice, we too can "tell the truth, but tell it slant."

31

The Strongest Friends of the Soul
There is no Frigate like a Book (1873)

There is no Frigate like a Book
To take us Lands away,
Nor any Coursers like a Page
Of prancing Poetry.
This Traverse may the poorest take
Without oppress of toll –
How frugal is the Chariot
That bears the Human Soul –

*F*or nine months in 1864, and seven more in 1865, Emily was sentenced to what might be called medical house arrest, away from her beloved Homestead. Her father sent her to stay with her Norcross cousins in Cambridgeport, Massachusetts, where she could be treated by a leading ophthalmologist in Boston for her worsening eye problems. It was, she later recalled, "a woe, that made me tremble." The treatments were painful, but what troubled her most was the doctor's order that she must not read:

> It was a shutting of all the dearest ones of
> time, the strongest friends of the soul –
> BOOKS. The medical man said avaunt ye
> book tormenters, he also said "down,

thought, & plunge into her soul." He
might as well have said, "Eyes be blind",
"heart be still."

When she was finally released and her deprivation ended,
her reaction was physical and visceral. She remembers: "Going
home I flew to the shelves and devoured the luscious passages. I
thought I should tear the leaves out as I turned them." Her prose
here is as metaphorical as her poetry. She doesn't describe it as
an intellectual exercise of the mind. It's as if she is physically gorg-
ing herself after a long period of starvation, reveling in the delec-
table food for the soul, reverting to instinct and almost
demolishing her sustenance in her eagerness.

Her Passion for Books

Almost a decade after her time of "woe" she wrote this
poem, her tribute to what she called "the strongest friends of
the soul" – her "BOOKS." As a young child she knew only
one book, the Bible, the only reading her father approved of
for his children. One day one of his law students was amazed
to learn that the children had nothing else to read, and he
started to bring them books, hiding them in a bush by the door.
She told her mentor, Thomas Higginson, how ecstatic she felt
after she found the first book: "This then is a book! And there
are more of them!"

In another poem, "Unto my Books – so good to turn," she
called them her "Kinsmen of the Shelf" – and eventually there
were a great many of them in the Dickinson household, more
than 900 titles. She had access to all of them. Her letters and
poems are filled with references and allusions to favorite authors,
most notably Elizabeth Barrett Browning and Robert Browning,
George Eliot, both Charlotte and Emily Bronte, Charles Dickens,
and her beloved Shakespeare, whom she valued above all. Her
bedroom, where she wrote most of her poetry, had three por-

traits on its walls. All were writers of books: Thomas Carlyle, Elizabeth Barrett Browning, and George Eliot.

Travel as a Metaphor

In "There is no Frigate like a Book," Dickinson chose travel – by ship (frigate), horse (courser), and carriage (chariot) – as a metaphor for books. They were vehicles for her soul. By 1873, when she wrote this poem, books had become the only way she traveled. Except for the two trips to the Boston area for her eye treatments, she had not been out of Amherst for thirteen years. Her last social visit away from home was in 1855. For the rest of her life, her books – along with her letters – continued to be her means of access to the outside world. In a letter dated 1882, a few years before her death, she was still acknowledging the power and vitality of books. She wrote: "A Book is the Heart's Portrait – every Page a Pulse."

The Flash of the Hummingbird
A Route of Evanescence (1879)

A Route of Evanescence,
With a revolving Wheel –
A Resonance of Emerald
A Rush of Cochineal –
And every Blossom on the Bush
Adjusts it's tumbled Head –
The Mail from Tunis – probably,
An easy Morning's Ride –

*B*y her own choice, Emily severely limited the number of human beings she came in contact with during her life. She felt differently, however, about birds. They were a welcome part of her garden world, the one place outside of her home where she felt totally comfortable. She found delight in their songs, in their movements, in the splash of color they added to her beloved natural world. They attracted and challenged her poetic imagination, so much so that she wrote fifty poems featuring birds. One species that regularly visited Emily's garden each summer was the hummingbird.

A Shared "Riddle" Poem
In 1879 she captured its essence in this poem. Emily must have been satisfied with it because it is one of the few that she

repeatedly sent to her friends – at least five of them received copies between 1879 and 1883. It is a "riddle" poem, a popular tradition that Dickinson occasionally followed. She must have been aware of the difficulty readers might have in guessing the poem's riddle because in each case, she identified its subject clearly to insure it would be understood.

One of the first to receive a copy was her fellow writer Helen Hunt Jackson, who apparently admired birds as much as Emily did. Helen and Emily had known each other when they were children and had later become literary friends through their letters. In one of them, Helen wrote, "I know your "Blue bird" by heart – and that is more than I do of any of my own verses . . . What should you think of trying your hand on the oriole?" In response, Emily wrote, "To the Oriole you suggested, I add a Humming Bird" and enclosed this poem.

A Signature and an Allegory

When Emily sent a copy to her Norcross cousins, the "answer" came in the form of the signature she affixed to the poem: "Humming bird." Helen Vendler believes this "signature" is not merely an identification of the subject of the poem; it serves also as an allegory of Dickinson herself as an artist. She "arrives, like the bird, quickly, vividly, and disturbingly, as she delivers, in her glittering linguistic plumage, her own exotic Mail."

Kinetic Imagery, Color, and Onomatopoeia

This poem has been described as a single "sustained metaphor." Like the bird it describes, it is tiny and elusive, "gone before it is fully comprehended." The poem has also been praised for its kinetic imagery. The poet captures the whirling movement of the little bird as it hovers briefly in midair before vanishing in a brilliant flash of color, leaving "tumbled" heads of flowers in its wake. Dickinson uses the ornithologically correct colors of green and red, but she renders them as the gemlike

"Emerald" and the exotic "Cochineal." In the family's 1828 Webster's dictionary, "cochineal" is defined as "a bright shade of red, scarlet or crimson." The soft whirring sound the bird makes is suggested in the repeated "r's" ("route," "resonance," and "rush") of its opening lines.

A Shakespearean Echo

Emily never chose to explain the last two lines in the poem, but readers have identified its source in Shakespeare's *The Tempest*. In a speech by Antonio in Act II, Scene 1, he notes that the "Queen of Tunis" cannot receive a note from Naples until morning. The allusion gives the hummingbird a role similar to that of a mailman who follows his route and completes his appointed tasks efficiently. Hummingbird watchers can readily recognize this image, given the bird's habit of returning regularly to its favorite feeding places at the same time each day.

A Painting of a Flower and a Poem about a Bird

Another friend who received a copy of this poem was Mabel Loomis Todd, a woman whose complex relationship with Emily's family remains one of the unresolved issues in Dickinson scholarship. She had a love affair for more than thirteen years with Austin, Emily's brother, while he was married to Emily's long-time friend Susan Gilbert, who was still living next door at the Evergreens.

In the fall of 1882, Mrs. Todd gave Emily a painting she had made of Indian pipes (the flower of the *Monotropa* plant). Emily responded by sending Mabel a copy of this poem with a note: "I know not how to thank you. . . . I cannot make an Indian Pipe but please accept a Humming Bird." By this time, Mabel had become a frequent visitor at the Homestead, where she played the piano and sang while Emily listened half-hidden from the hallway outside her upstairs room. Afterward, Emily would send in a poem, with sherry, cake, or a flower on a silver tray, but Emily and Mabel never met face-to-face. Emily kept the painting in her bedroom for the rest of her life.

An Affair and a First Edition

Austin and Mabel declared their love for each other at about the same time the painting/poem exchange took place. Soon afterward they began to use the Homestead as one of their meeting places for sexual intercourse. The affair continued until after Emily's death, but whether Emily ever realized its nature or extent remains an open question.

Emily's sister, Lavinia, later asked Mabel to help her publish Emily's poetry, and together with Thomas Higginson, Mabel co-edited the 1890 edition of Dickinson's poetry. That crucial event in the publishing history of Emily Dickinson's poetry can be partly traced to an exchange of a painting of a flower for this poem about a hummingbird.

The Lure of the Simple Life

How happy is the little Stone (1882)

How happy is the little Stone
That rambles in the Road alone,
And does'nt care about Careers
And Exigencies never fears –
Whose Coat of elemental Brown
A passing Universe put on,
And independent as the sun,
Associates or glows alone,
Fulfilling absolute Decree
In casual simplicity –

*E*mily continued to refuse to publish her poems all her life. Even those closest to her did not encourage her to publish – her family because they knew how adamant she was about not publishing and did not want to upset her; her mentor, Thomas Higginson, because he felt her poems were too eccentric to enter the literary marketplace. The only one of her contemporaries who not only recognized her genius but also urged her repeatedly to publish was her friend Helen Hunt Jackson, known in her day as the "greatest American woman writer." In a letter she wrote to Emily in 1876, she proclaimed:

> "You are a great poet – and it is wrong to
> the day you live in, that you will not sing

aloud. When you are what men call dead,
you will be sorry you were so stingy."

A Persistent Friend

Two years later, Helen succeeded in getting Emily to "sing aloud" when she convinced her to submit "Success is counted sweetest" to Thomas Niles, editor of a poetry anthology. Helen had assured her that all contributors would remain anonymous. Four years afterward, in 1882, Helen was again the instigator when Emily heard directly from Niles, who was with the publishing house of Roberts Brothers. He wrote:

> H. H. once told me that she wished you
> could be induced to publish a volume of
> poems. I should not want to say how highly
> she praised them, but to such an extent that
> I wish also that you could.

An Equally Persistent Poet

Emily proved to be as persistent in her refusals as Helen was in her inducements. In her reply to Niles, Emily wrote, "The kind but incredible opinion of 'H. H.' and yourself I would like to deserve – Would you accept a Pebble I think I gave her, though I am not sure."

If the message appeared enigmatic initially, once Niles read the "Pebble" poem that Emily enclosed with it, he would have had no doubt about her rejection of his offer to publish a volume of her poems. Under these circumstances, this poem becomes a clear statement of her desire not to pursue a career as a published poet.

Emily as the Stone

In this poem the speaker's admiration for the "little Stone" verges on envy. Emily's empathy with nature's creations, which are impervious to human concerns, dates as far back as 1856. She was twenty-five years old when she wrote, "I often wish I was a grass, or a toddling daisy, whom all these problems of the dust might not terrify." Twenty-five years later, when she wrote this poem, she was fifty-one. Her feelings had not changed, but now her envy is directed at an even more inanimate creation – a stone.

In this poem, the stone has often been interpreted as a metaphor for Dickinson's own life – that of a recluse finding fulfillment by quietly writing poems at home along with performing whatever daily duties her sister Lavinia chose to give her. As one reader put it, "The little stone's life of silence, casual simplicity and quiet independence exemplifies . . . the secluded, independent, soul-searching life of Emily Dickinson herself."

Emily's identification with her "pebble" extends to their physical appearance. Both are "little" in size and "elemental Brown" in color. She once described herself as "small, like the Wren" and added, "my hair is bold, like the Chestnut bur and the sherry in the Glass, that the Guest leaves." The colors she chose to describe herself were all assorted shades of "elemental Brown."

A Philosophical Statement – or Not

From a philosophical perspective, one reader detects an affiliation with Stoicism in the poem: an "indifference for the sort of goals for which human beings destroy their lives." In its place is the acceptance of a type of quiet happiness that Stoics promise. In a related view, the stone is seen as representing "harmony and integration within the self."

On the contrary, others say, the poem is filled with ironies. The stone lacks the crucial element of freedom: unlike human beings, it cannot "ramble" or exercise any significant options. Or bluntly put: "the trouble with the so-wholly satisfactory and adaptable object is that it is, after all, a soulless lump."

Playing with Ideas

Whether Dickinson meant this poem to be read ironically is a tricky question. Emily's poetry, like her mind, continually plays with ideas, examining them from one perspective and then another. Her poems do contradict each other because she uses them to explore both sides of a question. Readers can accept her admiration for the stone's way of life, or they can reject it and deem the poem ironic. But what they cannot deny is that the poem can be read as a rationale for her decision not to publish her poetry. It was a standpoint from which she seldom wavered.

34

God's Little Blond Blessing Gone
Pass to thy Rendezvous of Light (1883)

Pass to thy Rendezvous of Light,
Pangless except for us –
Who slowly ford the Mystery
Which thou hast leaped across!

*N*ew life arrived at the Evergreens – and into Emily's world – in 1875 when a new baby, Thomas Gilbert Dickinson, was born to Emily's brother, Austin, and his wife, Sue. Gib, as the family called him, was the youngest of their three children, born thirteen years after his brother, Ned, and nine years after his sister, Mattie. In her memoir, Martha Dickinson Bianchi remembers her little brother as a "willful and winsome child." "Being so much younger," she writes, "he grew up to be the idol of us all . . . One of his first rebellions was at the time someone tried to teach him to sing 'Home, sweet, sweet Home – there's no place like Home.'" He broke in to assert, "'Yes, there is, too! Over at my Aunt Emily's!'"

A Mutual Delight

Emily was thoroughly delighted by the latest addition to the family, and obviously he was delighted with her too. When Gib was two and a half years old, Emily proudly boasted to a friend about a clever remark her precocious nephew had made about "*Bumbul – Beese.*" He is, she added, "God's little Blond Blessing."

A letter Emily wrote to Gib when he was six years old captures the loving and whimsical relationship they shared:

> Gilbert asked a little plant of Aunt Emily,
> once, to carry to his Teacher – but Aunt
> Emily was asleep – so Maggie [the Dickin-
> son's servant] gave him one instead – Aunt
> Emily waked up now, and brought this little
> Plant all the way from her Crib for Gilbert to
> carry to his Teacher – Good Night – Aunt
> Emily's asleep again –

In another letter later the same year, Emily sent Gib something else to "carry to his Teacher": a poem entitled "The Bumble Bee's Religion," a homage of sorts to his early fascination with bees. The poem was accompanied by a dead bee! The following year, she sent him a short note with get-well wishes after he had an attack of croup: "Poor Little Gentleman, and so revered – ."

A Tragic Turn

This ongoing correspondence was brought to an abrupt and tragic end when Gib died unexpectedly and suddenly of typhoid fever at the age of eight. In the words of Emily's sister, Lavinia: "His fever was short & fierce & little more than one week ended his happy, brilliant life."

Emily was devastated by Gib's death. The night Gib died, Emily had overcome her deep-rooted antipathy to leaving the Homestead and gone next door to the Evergreens to check on his condition. It was a heart-breaking and wrenching experience. She describes it in a letter to one of her oldest and closest friends, Mrs. Holland:

> 'Open the Door, open the Door, they are
> waiting for me,' was Gilbert's sweet com-

mand in delirium. *Who* were waiting for
him, all we possess we would give to know –
Anguish at last opened it, and he ran to the
little Grave at his Grandparents' feet – All
this and more, though is there more? More
than Love and Death? Then tell me it's
name!

Shortly after Gib's death she wrote a letter to Sue. It included
"Pass to thy Rendezvous of Light."

Letter and Poem Entwined

Emily's letter to Sue is as much a release for her own grief
as it is an expression of sympathy for Sue. It is intended as consolation for both of them. Inadvertently, the letter offers a gloss
on the poem that was imbedded in it. The "Mystery" in the
poem's third line suggests the unknown supernatural world that
may or may not have awaited her nephew after his death. It also
reveals the unique, personal association the word "Mystery" had
for her because of the fun she and Gilbert had enjoyed with secrets. Emily shares that memory with Sue in the letter: "Gilbert
rejoiced in Secrets – His Life was panting with them – With what
menace of Light he cried 'Don't tell, Aunt Emily!' Now my as-
cended Playmate must instruct *me*."

The phrase "leaped across" in the fourth line of the poem
is paralleled by a sentence in the letter that describes how Emily
envisions him: " I see him in the Star, and meet his sweet velocity
in everything that flies." Gilbert's "velocity" alludes to how he
leaped through his fast-paced enjoyment of life. Her letter is filled
with the details that engulf her: "He knew no niggard moment –
His life was full of Boon – The playthings of the Dervish were not
so wild as his." The "leaped across" in the poem has another connotation as well; it encompasses the swiftness – a matter of a week
– with which he came down with the fever and then left them.

The Dark and the Light

The implicit contrast between light and dark in the poem is heightened in the letter. The poem focuses on Gilbert's passage into the "Rendezvous of Light." In the letter, he is "wronged only of Night, which he left for us." That is, the mourners are left in Night's darkness, but she finds some consolation in being able "to see him" in the light of a star.

Another opposition between the departed and those left behind can be found in the poem's depiction of Gilbert as "Pangless," that is, without the pangs of pain that clearly engulf her. The letter reinforces this positive view of the dead boy's new existence when Emily describes his "Requiem" as "ecstacy," a pleasurable extreme rather than a painful one. Emily's letter and her poem were intended to comfort her sister-in-law – and herself.

The Aftermath and a Postscript

According to her sister, Lavinia, Emily was "alarmingly ill for weeks" after Gib's death. Months later, she was still suffering from what her doctor called "Nervous Prostrations." Biographers agree that Emily never recovered completely from the shock of Gib's death.

Two years after Gib's death, she again included Gib's elegiac poem in another letter, this one to Thomas Higginson. She had sent a biography of George Eliot to Higginson after Eliot's death. She had long admired Eliot and mourned her death deeply. In her letter, she prefaced the poem with the statement: "Biography first convinces us of the fleeing of the Biographied." In sharing the esteemed writer's biography with her own literary mentor, Emily mourns her anew. She does so by using the elegy she had created at the "fleeing" of her beloved nephew Gib. His only biography was imprinted in the memory of those he left behind and eventually – for those who could understand it – in this poem.

The Blond Assassin at Play
Apparently with no surprise (1884)

Apparently with no surprise
To any happy Flower
The Frost beheads it at it's play –
In accidental power –
The blond Assassin passes on –
The Sun proceeds unmoved
To measure off another Day
For an Approving God –

*J*ust a year after the death of her beloved nephew Gib, Emily wrote this "apparently" detached observation of a killing frost. The poem sets up a striking parallel between the "blond Assassin" who "beheads" the "happy Flower" "at its play" and the fever that suddenly and swiftly killed the eight-year-old boy who had been her "little blond blessing" from God. It is anything but a dispassionate observation of a routine event in nature. Rather it is a triple condemnation: of the killer's "accidental power," of the "unmoved" sun which proceeds on its daily course, and of the "Approving God" who oversees it all.

This is not one of Emily Dickinson's celebrated poems. It was discovered after her death, jotted down on the back of an envelope addressed to her Aunt Elizabeth Currier. She never made a fair copy of it or included it in one of her fascicles, as she did with many other poems. But it is significant not only because it reveals the bewilderment and grief she continued to feel over Gib's death, but also because it shows how she returned to the same puzzling dilemma over the span of her lifetime. In it, she confronts anew the enigma she faced twenty-two years earlier in "A Bird came down the Walk": how to explain and accept the matter-of-fact brutality she witnessed in nature – and by extension, in the ongoing destruction of human life.

The germ for the specific metaphor at the center of this poem – the concept of God looking down approvingly each fall as the frost brutally kills the summer flowers – may have come from something the family gardener at the Homestead said to Emily's father. Two years before she wrote this poem, Emily wrote to her good friend Mrs. Holland about the gardener's death and reminisced about him:

> I remember he was at one time disinclined
> to gather the Winter Vegetables till they had
> frozen, and when Father demurred, he
> replied "Squire, ef the Frost is the Lord's
> Will, I don't popose to stan in the way of it."

Emily adds: "I hope a nearer inspection of that 'Will' has left him with as ardent a bias in it's favor." In making an ironic leap from the God who wills the frost that kills the vegetables to the Power that wills the death of the gardener, she anticipates the leap she makes implicitly in this poem. Both the frost that beheads the flower and the death that awaits all living things operate under the auspices of an "Approving God."

A Long-Standing Connection

But Dickinson had long been associating the death of plant life with the death of human life. In a letter written to the Hollands almost two decades earlier in November 1858, during a fever epidemic in Amherst, Emily expresses her distress about the prevalence of death around her:

> I can't stay any longer in a world of death.
> Austin is ill of fever. I buried my garden last
> week – our man, Dick, lost a little girl
> through the scarlet fever . . . Ah! Demo-
> cratic Death! Grasping the proudest zinnia
> from my purple garden, – then deep to his
> bosom the serf's child.

Emily's mourning over the death of flowers goes back even further to her childhood. As a child, she was able to find solace in the teachings of Edward Hitchcock, a geologist and educator at Amherst College. In a letter to Higginson, she explained: "When Flowers annually died and I was a child, I used to read Dr. Hitchcock's Book on the Flowers of North America. This comforted their Absence – assuring me they lived."

A Child No More

But when she wrote this poem, she was far from being a child. She was fifty-three years old, and only two years away from her own death. She had found it increasingly difficult to reconcile the cycle of death and rebirth in nature with the cycle of death and resurrection in humans, because the evidence of rebirth for humans could not so easily be confirmed. At this point in her life, she had suffered the loss of many of her loved ones. In this poem, she wonders anew what to make of the role the "Approving God" plays in all that slaughter.

36

The Final Confrontation

My life closed twice before it's close (Undated)

My life closed twice before it's close;
It yet remains to see
If immortality unveil
A third event to me,

So huge, so hopeless to conceive
As these that twice befell.
Parting is all we know of heaven,
And all we need of hell.

*I*mmortality was Emily Dickinson's "flood" subject, as she herself claimed, but immortality's precursor – death – dominated her life and her poetry to an equal extent. When still a child, before she was old enough to conceive of immortality, she lived with a mother who communicated her "tremulous fear of death" to all her children. From the time Emily was nine until she was twenty-four, she lived in a house on North Pleasant Street, adjacent to the village burial ground, where she could see funeral processions pass by as a routine occurrence and as a constant reminder of the omnipresence of death. Her own life was filled with the death of loved ones. Lavinia summed up a pattern in her sister's life when she remembered, after Emily's own death, how often she had seen her "cut to the heart when death robbed her again and again."

Three Early Losses

The earliest of these traumatic losses occurred in 1884, when Emily was thirteen. She was part of a death watch at the bedside of her young friend Sophia Holland. The experience affected her so profoundly that she became ill and was sent away to stay with relatives for a month to recuperate. In 1850, Emily grieved over the death of Leonard Humphrey, her tutor from Amherst College, who was not much older than herself and whom she admired greatly. And in 1853, she lost another close friend and mentor; Ben Newton had been a law student in her father's office, and they had corresponded regularly. Ben's death is most often suggested as the trigger for the poem "I never lost as much but twice" written in 1858. His is the final death in the trilogy that leads to that poem's blasphemous finale.

More Losses Later

Deaths with a major impact on Emily continued long after 1853:

- In 1874, her father died. Emily became physically ill after his death. She described the trauma she felt in agonizing detail in a letter to Thomas Higginson: "His Heart was pure and terrible and I think no other like it exists."
- In 1878, Samuel Bowles died. He and Emily shared a friendship that began in the early 1850s, in the course of which they wrote to each other often and she sent him thirty-seven of her poems. Some think her mysterious "Master" letters were meant for him.
- In 1880, the Reverend Charles Wadsworth died. Emily called him her "closest earthly friend." He also has been proposed as the intended recipient of her "Master" letters. His death prompted a correspondence with Wadsworth's close friends, the Clark brothers. She wrote a total of twenty-one letters to them, the last one sent during her own final days.
- In 1883, her beloved eight-year-old nephew Gib died. Her grief

once again made her dangerously ill. Its devastation is expressed in the letter she wrote to her sister-in-law and the poem she included in it: "Pass to thy Rendezvous of Light."

• In 1884, Judge Otis Phillips Lord died. In him, Emily had found at last the lover she had long fantasized about. Emily's letters to him confirm a mutual and fulfilling love they found in each other late in their lives. Later that year Emily wrote: "The Dyings have been too deep for me, and before I could raise my Heart from one, another has come."

Her Own Near-Death Experience

Emily had a close encounter with death herself in August 1884. She described it in a letter to her Norcross cousins:

> Eight Saturday noons ago, I was making a
> loaf of cake with Maggie, when I saw a great
> darkness coming and knew no more until
> late at night. I woke to find Austin and Vin-
> nie and a strange physician bending over
> me, and supposed I was dying, or had died,
> all was so kind and hallowed. I had fainted
> and lain unconscious for the first time in my
> life. Then I grew very sick and gave the oth-
> ers much alarm, but am now staying. The
> doctor calls it "revenge of the nerves"; but
> who but Death had wronged them?

Although she could not have known it, she would die two years later. She may, however, have had a premonition of it. That traumatic event, combined with the death of Judge Lord earlier that same year and preceded by the death of her nephew Gib the year before, appear to fit the circumstances described in "My life closed twice before it's close."

The temptation to interpret the poem biographically is irresistible, but in spite of the circumstantial evidence, such a reading remains conjectural. The fact is that scholars have been unable to determine when Dickinson wrote this poem. Consequently, the identity of the two "partings" cannot be established with certainty. The evidence is merely circumstantial. She had strong emotional ties to each of the five departed listed above, all of whom died between 1874 and 1884; the deaths of any two of them could have triggered the thought of the close of her own life. Ultimately, the specific identity doesn't matter. What is significant is the effect these cumulative losses had on her.

Three Closures and a Recurring Question

The opening line refers to the close of the speaker's life, which suggests that Dickinson wrote this poem when her own death was on her mind. This would certainly have been the case in 1884 when she had her near-death experience. But, as the long list of the loved ones she lost makes clear, death was a continual presence. Her most famous poem about dying, "Because I could not stop for Death," was written in 1862, midway through her life, not near its end. Readers can choose which two specific losses she is referring to – or they can view the two closures as a synthesis of all the grief she had endured and a prequel to the closure of her own life.

In this poem, she is once again facing her "flood subject, immortality" and wondering what it will "unveil" for her when her own life closes. Establishing a significant caveat with the word "If" in the third line, she considers the possibility that her death will not be as "huge" and "hopeless" as the losses that "twice befell" her when her loved ones died. She appears to be hoping to discover that immortality does exist. In the last two lines, she evokes the "heaven" and the "hell" associated with the traditional Christian afterlife, but only to place them squarely in the life experienced on earth. The penultimate line could be interpreted as suggesting that we know "heaven" when, in parting with our loved ones, we fully recall and appreciate the happiness we shared with them when they were alive. This parting would then be seen as a preview of what's in store if heaven truly exists. In the last line, we know "hell" when we experience the pain of having lost the departed and the fear of never being reunited because there may be no life after death. Here the poet leaves us, the readers, with the possibility of both and the certainty of neither.

The Final Confrontation

One of Dickinson's biographers, Cynthia Woolf, resolves the ambiguity of this poem: she believes that in it, the poet sees "the full barrenness of human fate" not as a "personal grievance" but as "a universal tragedy." In fact, at the end of Woolf's extended and detailed account of Dickinson's life and poetry, she concludes, along with many other Dickinson scholars, that when the poet actually faced her own death, she had made peace with the God she earlier rebelled against.

The last letter Emily wrote was addressed to her "Little Cousins," Louise and Frances Norcross, and contained only two words: "Called back." Emily had read Hugh Conway's "sentimental, spiritual" novel *Called Back*, and Woolf sees the meaning of her final note as "entirely clear": it was "an expression of confidence about the realm that awaited her." Others have thought otherwise.

Emily Dickinson died on May 15, 1886, at the Homestead. The official diagnosis was Bright's disease, a kidney disorder. She was buried in the family plot in Amherst Cemetery. In the early twentieth century, the poet's niece, Martha Dickinson Bianchi replaced the original gravestone, which bore just her initials, "EED," and chose for her epitaph the last words Emily ever wrote:

"CALLED BACK."

✦ Chronology ✦

*T*his chronology is intended as a corollary to the events covered in the chapters of this book and therefore contains only facts pertinent to the portions of Emily Dickinson's life that are relevant to the 36 poems included in it. My book is meant to serve as an introduction to the complex life of a complicated poet, using 36 of her 1,789 poems as entry points. Many other equally essential aspects of her life and her world are necessarily omitted, as is the remaining bulk of her poetry.

1828: Emily Dickinson's parents, Edward Dickinson and Emily Norcross, are married.

1829: Emily's brother, Austin, is born on April 16.

1830: Emily's parents and Austin move to the Homestead in Amherst, Massachusetts.
Emily Elizabeth Dickinson is born on December 10 at the Homestead.
Emily's future "best" friend and sister-in-law, Susan Gilbert, is born on December 19.

1831: Emily's mother joins Amherst's Congregational Church.

1833: Emily's sister, Lavinia, is born on February 28.

1835: Emily starts attending the district's primary school.
Emily's father becomes treasurer of Amherst College.

1838: Emily's father is elected to the Massachusetts legislature.

1840: The Dickinson family moves to North Pleasant Street in Amherst.
Emily and Lavinia attend Amherst Academy.

1842: Emily's father is elected to the Massachusetts legislature for a second term.

1844: Emily is sent to visit relatives in Boston and Worcester after Sophia Holland's death.

1846: Emily writes to Abiah Root describing her death-watch over Sophia Holland.

1847: Emily enters Mount Holyoke Female Seminary and remains for one year.

1849: Emily becomes friends with Susan Gilbert.

1850: Emily begins her correspondence with Susan Gilbert.
Emily writes a rhymed satiric valentine letter printed in an Amherst College publication.
Emily's father and sister join Amherst's Congregational Church during a revival.
Susan Gilbert joins Amherst's Congregational Church.
Emily's friend and tutor Leonard Humphrey dies.

1852: Emily writes several love letters to Susan Gilbert.
Emily sends a comic valentine poem to her father's law partner.
Emily's father is elected to Congress.

1853: Emily's "Preceptor" and close friend Ben Newton dies.
Emily's brother and her friend Susan Gilbert become secretly engaged.

1854: Emily writes to Abiah Root declining her invitation to visit her.

1855: Emily and her sister visit Washington, D.C., and Philadelphia.
Emily meets the Reverend Charles Wadsworth in Philadelphia.
The Dickinson family moves back to the Homestead.

1856: Emily's brother joins Amherst's Congregational Church.
Emily's brother and Susan Gilbert marry.
The newlyweds move to the house next door, the Evergreens, that Austin's father built for them.
Emily becomes friends with Samuel Bowles through Austin and Susan.

1857: Emily ignores Emerson's lecture in Amherst and his overnight visit at the Evergreens.

1858: Emily writes 43 poems, including
"One sister have I in the house": Chapter 2;
"I never lost as much but twice": Chapter 3.
Emily begins gathering her poems into fascicles.
Emily writes the draft of the first "Master" letter.

1859: Emily writes 82 poems, including
"Success is counted sweetest": Chapter 4;
"Safe in their Alabaster Chambers": Chapter 5.

1860: Emily writes 54 poems, including
"Did the Harebell loose her girdle": Chapter 6.
Wadsworth visits Emily at the Homestead.
Emily makes her last social visit away from Amherst.

1861: Emily writes 88 poems, including
"Wild nights – wild nights!": Chapter 1;
"'Faith' is a fine invention": Chapter 7;
"Come slowly – Eden!": Chapter 8;
"I taste a liquor never brewed": Chapter 9;
"Some keep the Sabbath going to Church": Chapter 10;
"I'm Nobody! Who are you?": Chapter 11.
"I taste a liquor never brewed" is published anonymously
in the *Republican* without her permission.
Emily writes the drafts of the second and third "Master" letters.
Samuel Bowles becomes seriously ill.
Emily experiences a "terror" that she never explains.
The Civil War begins.

1862: Wadsworth moves to San Francisco to accept a new position
at Calvary Church.
Sam Bowles travels in Europe for health reasons.
Emily writes 227 poems, including
"'Hope' is the thing with feathers": Chapter 12;
"There's a certain Slant of light": Chapter 13;
"Before I got my eye put out": Chapter 14;
"I felt a Funeral, in my brain": Chapter 15;
"A Bird, came down the Walk": Chapter 16;
"I cannot dance opon my Toes": Chapter 17;
"I like to see it lap the Miles": Chapter 18;
"The Soul selects her own Society": Chapter 19;
"Mine – by the right of the White Election!": Chapter 20;
"Because I could not stop for Death": Chapter 21.
"Safe in their Alabaster Chambers" is published
anonymously without her permission in the *Republican*.
Emily sends her first letter and four poems to her future life-
long mentor, Thomas Higginson.
Emily's nephew Ned is born to Susan and Austin.

1863: Emily writes 295 poems, including
"This is my letter to the World": Chapter 22;
"I heard a Fly buzz – when I died": Chapter 23;
"The Brain – is wider than the Sky": Chapter 24;
"Much Madness is divinest Sense": Chapter 25;
"I started Early – Took my Dog": Chapter 26;
"I cannot live with You": Chapter 27.

1864: Emily writes 98 poems, including
"I never saw a Moor": Chapter 28.
Emily stays in Boston area with Norcross cousins while under
going painful eye treatments.
"Some keep the Sabbath going to Church" is published
anonymously in *The Round Table* without her permission.
Emily contributes to the Civil War fund-raising effort by giving
permission for the anonymous publication of four of her
poems: "Success is counted sweetest" in the *Brooklyn
Daily Union* and three others in *Drum Beat*.

1865: Emily writes 229 poems, including
"A narrow Fellow in the Grass": Chapter 29.
Emily returns to her cousins in Boston area to receive more
eye treatments.
Emily returns to the Homestead, blindness averted, and begins
her life as a confirmed recluse.
The Civil War ends.
Emily's dog, Carlo, dies.

1866: Emily continues writing to Wadsworth, attempting to keep
their correspondence secret.
"A narrow Fellow in the Grass" is published anonymously and
without her permission in the *Republican*.
Emily's niece, Martha, is born to Susan and Austin.

1870: Higginson visits Emily at the Homestead for the first time.

1872: Emily writes 35 poems, including
"Tell all the truth but tell it slant": Chapter 30.

1873: Emily writes 38 poems, including
"There is no Frigate like a Book": Chapter 31.
Emily's father is elected to the General Court of Massachusetts.
Emily is examined, at her father's request, by the Rev. Jenkins,
who finds her spiritually "sound."
Higginson visits Emily at the Homestead for the second and
last time.

1874: Emily's father dies unexpectedly in Boston.

1875: Her nephew Gilbert ("Gib") is born to Susan and Austin.

1878: Helen Hunt Jackson convinces her to publish "Success is
counted sweetest" anonymously.

1879: Emily writes 35 poems, including
"A Route of Evanescence": Chapter 32.

1880: Wadsworth visits Emily at the Homestead for the second and final time.

Judge Lord's wife dies.

1881: Emily and Judge Lord exchange love letters.

Judge Lord visits Emily at the Homestead regularly.

1882: Emily writes 27 poems, including
"How happy is the little Stone": Chapter 33.

Austin and Mabel Loomis Todd begin their love affair.

Wadsworth dies.

Judge Lord becomes seriously ill.

1883: Emily's beloved eight-year-old nephew "Gib" dies.

Emily writes 34 poems, including
"Pass to thy Rendezvous of Light": Chapter 34.

Emily becomes very ill.

1884: Emily writes 42 poems, including
"Apparently with no surprise": Chapter 35.

Judge Lord dies.

Emily becomes very ill again.

(Undated: Emily writes "My life closed twice before it's close":
Chapter 36.)

1886: Emily dies on May 15.

1890: Mabel Todd and Higginson edit the first of three series of
Poems by Emily Dickinson published by Roberts Brothers.

✦ Backnotes for Sources ✦
by Paragraphs

*T*he text of all of Dickinson's poems are from *The Poems of Emily Dickinson*, edited by R. W. Franklin. The first backnote for each chapter uses the abbreviation F for the Franklin source and J for the number assigned in the 1960 Thomas Johnson edition. *Letters* is the abbreviation used for Johnson's edition of Dickinson's letters.

Chapter 1: The "Virgin Recluse" Breaks a Taboo

1: *Wild nights – Wild nights!* : F269/J249

2. "One poem only": Bingham, *Ancestors* 127; "My life has": *Letters* #330, 2:460

4: "How easy quite" Franklin, *Master Letters* 16; "A love so": Franklin, *Master Letters* 22; "Master – open your" : Franklin, *Master Letters* 23

5: "I am older": Franklin, *Master Letters* 35, 43-44

6: Samuel Bowles supported by Sewall, Wolff, and Farr; Charles Wadsworth supported by Habegger and Pollak

7: "I am distressed": Wolff 389

8: "There came a day", "intense farewell scene": Habegger 412-13

9: a gossip's version: Leyda 34

10: another with no surviving documentation: Habegger 411; one psychoanalytic critic: Cody

11: assumes role of male lover: Todd 36-37, Marcus 57-58, Reed 283-84; both lovers are women: Faderman 20-26, n.5; homoerotic partner is Susan Gilbert; their letters of greater significance than the Master letters: Hart xii, xiv. Also see Chapter 2 about "One sister have I in the house."

12: "voluptuousness in the": Wolff 383; imagery and metaphor: Day 210; Mc Neil 15; Wolff 383

13: subjunctive mood: Juhasz, "Dwell in Possibility" 108-09; plural form: Wegelin 25

Chapter 2: A Sister Like No Other

1: *One Sister have I in the house – :* F5/J14

2: "I think of love": Hart 24; "And now how soon": Hart 30-34

2: "facilitating confidante": Habegger 305

3: Emily's first known letter to Sue in 1850: Hart xxxii, 7

4: "early, earnest, indissoluble": *Letters* #827, 3:779; "The tie between us": Hart 261;

5: "It is weird": Habegger 359-60

7: Sue and Emily both born in December 1830: Hart xxxi; had begun sharing poems with Sue in 1853: Hart 44; Sue absorbed by her separate past and interior life: Habegger 360

8: allegiance to Sue: Habegger 360; 276 poems: Wolff 176; : Emily changing a poem: See Chapter 5 on *Safe in their Alabaster Chambers*

9: For extensive and detailed account of this poem's publication history, see Gordon

10: fascicle version inked over: Hart 77; out of respect for Austin's wishes: Bingham, *Ancestors* viii

11: published in 1914: Bianchi, *Single Hound*

Chapter 3: God as a Serial Killer

1: *I never lost as much but twice*: F39/J49

2: "It seemed to": Habegger 172

3: "I have never": *Letters* #11, 1: 32

4: " a young man": Sewall 2: 340; "excellent Principal": Lease in Eberwein 141; "I write Abiah": *Letters* #39, 1:102

5: "gentle, yet grave": *Letters* #153, 1:282 –83

7: quoting from Ben's letter: *Letters* #457, 3:551-52

8: death of 33 young people: Bingham 179-80

9: "a liar, a betrayer ": Lewis, R. W. B. "Foreword" in Wolff xix; "an expression of faith": Lackey 18; "a cry of": Lambert 16

10: "the Biblical view": deFord, 24. Others have rejected such an approach: Pollak ("'That Fine Prosperity,'" 168-69) feels this "economic formulation" serves to deflate "the significance of the poet's own emotion; Machor (131-46) believes it would dilute Dickinson's frustration with conventional attitudes of feminine resignation. Other feminist oriented critics: Leder and Abbott

11: "He buys me" : *Letters* #261. See also Mossberg: "like her own father, God is seen to be creating her dependence upon him at the same time that he sadistically refuses to satisfy her needs"; "His Heart was": Johnson, *Letters* 418, 2:528

13: "without her struggle": Paglia 87

Chapter 4: From Kitchen Sink to a Civil War Batttlefield

1: *Success is counted sweetest*: F112/J67; source for this poem: Sewall, *Life* 2:387; "On the lounge": *Letters* #36, 1: 97-98

5: "It feels a shame to be Alive": F524; mistaken assumptions by Edmund Wilson: Biscella 46-47; Ford; Wolosky

6: "War feels to": *Letters* #280, 2:423

7: publication in *Drum Beat*: Dandurand 89

8: "I ask it": *Letters* #573b, 2:625

9: thought the poem was written by Emerson: *Letters* #2: 626-27; "so white": Bianchi, *Face to Face*. 30

10: "superiority of defeat": Wilbur 40-41

11: "I smile when": *Letters* 265, 2:408

Chapter 5: Taking and Defying Advice

1: *Safe in their alabaster chambers*: F124/J216; began sharing poems with Sue: Hart 44; "Dear Sue ": *Letters* #757, 3:733

2: "ghostly shimmer": *Letters* #238, 2:379-380.

3: "If I read a book": *Letters* 2:473-74

4: laughing breezes, babbling bees: published in Johnson, *Poems* 100: "Light laughs the breeze / In her Castle above them – / Babbles the Bee in a stolid Ear, / Pipe the Sweet Birds in ignorant cadence"; "Perhaps this verse:" *Letters* #238, 2:379-380; "not suited": ibid; "Could I make": ibid

7: entombed dead are the Elect: Dietrich 96; "Blessed are the meek": Matthew 5:5; stone burial vault: Abbott,"Safe'" 139.

Chapter 6: "Did the harebell loose her girdle"

1: *Did the Harebell loose her girdle*: F134/J213

2: her gentleman caller in1860: Eberwein vxi

3: Wadsworth relationship: See Chapter 1 "Wild nights"; "Wonder
     stings" : Franklin, *Master Letters* 26

6: childlike qualities: Walker 105-06

7. description of harebell: Farr, *Gardens* 185; 400 references to flowers:
     Bennett,"Flowers" 116; bee on 124 occasions, Fegan 160

8: "dread of generalized ": Griffith,"Him" 20; "lover's physical desire":
     Cody 371-72; "lovely, lost vamp": Keller 25-26

9: pearl as clitoral image: Bennett 167; biblical source: Vendler 45-46

10: humor, coquette: Walker 65-66

Chapter 7: Faith and Microscopes

1: *Faith is a Fine Invention*: F202/J185; read "every night": *Letters*
     # 133, 1:264

2: met through Austin and Sue: Wolff 248

3: good times next door: Wolff 248

4: "Once when he had driven ": Bianchi, *Face to Face* 62

5: Bowles played a major role : Sewall, Wolff, Farr *Passion*; good
     friends: Habegger, Pollak *Guide*

6: share 37of her poems: Wolff 248

7: in a letter to Samuel Bowles: Leyda 2:7; Bowles' series of physical
     collapses: Habegger 426: "boils & bowels" Habeger 423

8: Bowles was a secular man: Wolff 248; "Patience & Faith," "Faith
     I find": Habegger 423;

9: strong grounding in science: Wolff viii-xix; Sewall, *Life* 478-79;
     Habegger 415; science as supportive adjunct to religion: Wolff
     xviii-xix

10: Juxtaposing a generalization: Short 9, Lair 14, 34; faith in same
     invention category: Fry 21-31

Chapter 8: Making Merry with Bumblebees

1: *Come slowly – Eden*: F205/J 211

2: "Austin wanted me": Habegger 186

3: probably unconscious eroticism: Habegger 187

4: definition of "Bashful": Webster's 1828 Dictionary, Electronic
   Version by Christian Technologies, Inc.

5. jasmine as a tropical flower: Farr, *Gardens* 55; jasmine grown
   in Emily's convervatory in "icy New England": Farr *Gardens*
   159. also *Letters* 3:655; definitions of "nectar" and
   "balm": ibid Webster's.

6: "wonderful yet deadly," Juhasz 25; "precarious balance between":
   Porter 112-13

7: confusion of gender roles, Salska, 135-40; Pollak 113; "male
   experience of": Challiff 94

8: "When I state ": *Letters* 268, 2:412; "to say if": ibid 260, 2:403

Chapter 9: Getting Drunk on Nature

1: *I taste a liquor never brewed* : F207/ J214 ;"It's a glorious":
   Letters 80, 1:187

2: "better that the college": Habegger 241; humorous fable: Anderson, *Stairway* 73-75

4: Emerson's "Bacchus" as source: Stewart 70, Capps 114-16;
   echoes of Emerson's "The Poet": Leyda 2:20; Emerson's
   transcendentalism different from Emily's union with nature:
   Day 213; delirious state of happiness: Morey, *Hundred Best*

5: beer instead of wine: Lambert 14-15. In an earlier draft of the
   poem, the "Frankfort" line was originally "Not all the vats
   upon the Rhine," similarly connecting the intoxicating bever-
   age with Germany and beer.

6: "nonsensical faulty rhyme": Anonymous, "The Newest Poet";
   editors altered lines: Sewall, *Life* 2:489; lack of control now
   viewed as enhancing: Raab 290, Wolff 187

7: excellent example: Johnson, "Textual Notes" 14; the reel: Wolff
   187; abcb rhyme of hymns: DeJong 152

8: "effervescent magic": Miller 151-52; "dazzling": Taggard 13

Chapter 10: The Good Little Girl Rebels

1: *Some keep the Sabbath going to church*: F236 /J324; "One
   Sunday": Leyda 1:478

2: stopped going to church: Todd, VI 114; also see Franklin 236,
   Johnson 324

3: "The cordiality of ": Sewall, *Life* 1:269, Appendix II; "I say unto you ": Johnson, *Letters* #432, 2:537

4: "I am at home": *Letters* # 54, 1:140; "They will all go": *Letters* #77, 1:181; "I will write": *Letters* #80, 1:187

5: "It is Sunday": *Letters* #184, 2:327

6: "if God had": *Letters* #185, 2:329; "Earth is Heaven": #1435, Franklin, *Poems* 543

7: Dickinson had read Emerson: Capps 112; "I do not respect 'doctrines'": *Letters* #200, 2:346

8: ten published during her lifetime: Pollak 16; The editor of the journal that printed it was Charles Sweetser, Emily's cousin by marriage, who had probably received it from someone in the family. It was printed with the title "My Sabbath" in the March 12, 1864, edition of the New York journal *The Round Table*: Scholnick

8: "the characteristic meter": Stephenson 280-81. The eighteenth-century mystic William Blake also employs a similar childlike rhythm and tone while undercutting the trappings of Christianity, but no evidence has been found that she was familiar with his writings: Eberwein 23-24

9: the two preachers: Towheed 23-24

10: irony at the core: Rieke 26

Chapter 11: Being Nobody, But Not Really

1: *I'm Nobody! Who are you?*: F260 / J288;"elfing it": Bianchi, *Face to Face* 63

2: last social visit: Pollak, Guide 245

3: "Odd, that I who say 'No'": Leyda 2:41

4: Yankee humor: Wallace 19; politicians and ministers: Wolff 194

5: "Nobody" is the real "Somebody": Moseley 12, Todd 9-10;"there is always one thing": *Letters* #405, 2:519 (as quoted by Higginson in letter to his sister)

6: Charles Mackay's "Little Nobody" as source: Sewall, *Life* 2:674

7: early defense: Alexander 66-67; self-exile: Rao 58

Chapter 12: The Bird of Hope

1: *Hope is the thing with feathers*: F314/J254 ; "Somehow I am ": *Letters* #123, 1:249

2: a "terror" in her life": *Letters* #261, 2:404; See Franklin, *Master Letters*

3: "sense of isolation": Habegger 436

4:"a violent attack": Habegger 424; more letters than ever before: Appendix 3 in *Letters* 3: 961

5: "I send you this": Habegger 436

6: "We differ often": *Letters* #173, 1:305-06

7: "In a serener Bright ": Franklin, *Poems* # 4

8: read *Springfield Republican*: Whicher 270; "Mrs. Adams had news": *Letters* #245, 2:386

Chapter 13: The Light of Despair

1: *There's a certain slant of light* : F320/J258

2: under category of nature: Anderson, *Stairway* 216

3: year and day ending: Perrine 34; short afternoons in winter: Thackrey 36

4: "I visited her often": *Letters* #11, 1:32 (See Chapter 3, "I never lost as much but twice")

5: "I told no one": *Letters* #11, 1:32; *Letters* #381, 2:501

6: no one has surpassed: Sewall, *Life* 2:611; "directness, dignity" :Winters 294

7: "Light compared to": Thackrey 36

8: "weight of great": Johnson, *Biography* 190; changed "heft" to "weight," Johnson, *Complete Poems* ix

9: the dictionary she used regularly: *Letters* #261, 2:404; definition of "heft" applied to "despair":Anderson, *Stairway* 216-17 "an oblique reflection": Anderson, *Stairway* 217; religious associations: Cunningham 456; deepen the despair: Pickard 69-70; "Flood subject": *Letters* #319

10: "external natural world and internal psychic experience": Spear 283

Chapter 14: Punctuaring the Cornea with a Needle

1: *Before I got my eye put out* : F336/J327; detailed account of Dickinson's eye problems, diagnosis, and treatment: Hirschhorn 300-09; "the calls at": *Letters* #289, 2:430;

2: diagnosis of iritis/uveitis: Hirschhorn 303; "Eyes once bright":

Hirschhorn 306; danger of permanent blindness: Hirschhorn 303; "a woe, the only one": Sewall, *Lyman Letters* 76

3: permanently recaptures nature through language: Phillips 73-74

5: "I have been sick": *Letters* #296, 2:435; "I have not looked": *Letters* #289, 2:430

6: "by signal at": Bianchi, *Face to Face* 30, 11; "The snow light": *Letters* #302, 2:439

7: one of her biographers: Wolff 164-65; another scholar: Guthrie; 849 poems: Franklin, *Poems* 639

Chapter 15: A Creak Across the Soul
1: *I felt a funeral, in my brain* : F340/J 280; "I had a terror": *Letters* #261, 2:404

2: eye problems: Hirschhorn; Wadsworth's move to California: Habegger 421, fn.1

3: "an emotional upheaval": Cody 191; agoraphobia: Garbowsky 152

4: panic attack, "the physical sensations . . . ": McDermott, 77

5: superficially about funerals: Monteiro 656-63

6: follows stages of a Congregationalist funeral: Wolff 228; "narrative center" missing: Wolff 232

7: tactile, auditory and kinetic images: Cambon 127-28

9: "We both believe": the basis for McIntosh's book on how Dickinson uses her vacillations between doubt and faith in her poetry

10: "She seems as": Sewall, *Life* 2:502

Chapter 16: Eating the Fellow Raw
1: *A bird came down the walk*: F359/J328; "wonderful . . . the air full": *Letters* #157, 1:288; "out in the new": *Letters* #184, 2:184

2: No fewer than fifty: Ando 22

3: "motion through space": Frankenberg 240; ugliness and beauty at the same time: Alexander 74-75; "nature's impenetrable enigma": Wolff 487-488

4: "destructive core": Pickard 61-62

5: wordplay: McCann 4

6: disjunction: Christanne Miller, "Disjunction" 85

7: poet as observer, Bouson 37; nature's indifference: Ferlazzo 104-106.

8: birds as creatures of another world: Anderson, *Stairway* 117-19

Chapter 17: No Pirouettes for Her

1: *I cannot dance opon my Toes*: F381/J326; "Are you too": *Letters* #260; for an excellent book-length account of the relationship between Emily and Higginson, see Brenda Wineapple's *White Heat*.

2: "you called me 'Wayward'": *Letters* #271, 2:415; "You think my gait 'spasmodic'": *Letters* #265, 2:409: "wince": *Letters* #268; "I have had": *Letters* #269; "Obedience": *Letters* #268, 2:412

3: "I thank you, "more orderly," "I shall observe, "never consciously touch," "I do not": *Letters* #271: 2:415; asserts her confidence: Galparin 116; refuses to copy the skills of others: Julia Walker 20

4: "artifice of ballet to satirize the artifice of conventional poetry": Anderson, *Stairway* 21-24

6: exhibitionism: Pollak, *Anxiety* 239-40

7: "dazzling display": Wolff 187; lines alternate evoking dancer's leaps: Leder and Abbott 185-86; also see Mossberg 156-58

8: "Did I displease": *Letters* 274, 2:417; "You were so": *Letters* 282, 2:425

9: stopped asking for advice from Higginson: Sewall, *Life* 2:560 ; "I do not": *Letters* #271, 2:415

Chapter 18: The Iron Horse of Amherst

1: *I like to see it lap the miles*: F383/J585 ; "New London is": *Letters* #126, 1: 253; "The New London": *Letters* #127, 1:254

2: "the most beautiful": Habagger 297; arguing for the Massachusetts Central Railroad: Sewall *Life* 1:54-55 "Since we have": *Letters* #72, 1:173; "While I write": *Letters* #123, 1: 250

3: "Since we have ": *Letters* #72, 1:173; "While I write": *Letters* #123, 1:250

4: "accidents where railroads": *Letters* #133, 1:264

5: a comic poem: Oberhaus 119-20; the conceit of the galloping horse: Pickard 76-77

6: "Austin loved excitement": Bianchi, *Face to Face* 129-30

7: "riddle" poem: Lucas 43-44

8: Shakespeare's "sound and fury": *Macbeth* Act V, Scene 5

9: Anderson, *Stairway* 14-16

10: "I like to *hear* it": Sewall, *Life* 2:437, n. 6; "It sounds so": *Letters* #140, 1:269

11: Boanarges allusion: Mark 3:17; Apostles John and James's tempestuous temper: Luke 9:54; "Sons of Thunder": Anderson, *Stairway* 16; "any declamatory": Webster's 1828 Dictionary, Electronic Version by Christian Technolgies, Inc.

12: Domnhall Mitchell, 1-26, adds the caveat that Dickinson "likes" the nineteenth-century's icon of progress only so long as she can use language to control it; Oberhaus 119-20

Chapter 19: Choosing Friends Deliberately
1: *The soul selects her own society*: F409/J303; "Hills – Sir – and": *Letters* #261, 2:404; "shunning Men": *Letters* #271, 2: 415

3: "I don't go": *Letters* #166, 1:298-99

4: "are not like": *Letters* #118, 1:245; "we're all unlike": *Letters* #114

5: "As for Emily": Bingham, *Home* 413-14

6: "I never was": *Letters* #2:476

7: one biographer, Habegger 451

8: "My friends are my": *Letters* #193, 2:338; "My friends are few": *Letters* #223. 2:366; one friend at a time: Brooks 2:1243-44

10: the art of poetry: Kher 257; chose seclusion: Rich 51; "her most dazzingly": Eberwein xvi, "1862"; also see Sewall, *Life* 72-73, 75 and Luscher 111-16

11: "higher and more": Morey, "Hundred Best" 37-38; "The greatest Saints": Capps 61

12: Calvinists' insistence: Westbrook 60; "As the soul ": Hecht 17-18

13: ; "astounding pride": Savage 752; becomes its own tomb: Duncan 124-25; "too far to": Jumper 5

15:: "But why should": Leyda 2:272-73

Chaper 20: The Power of White

1: *Mine - by the Right of the White Election!*: F411/J528; "During my memory": Bianchi, *Face to Face* 16-17; Lyman remembers: Farr *The Gardens* 69; "her dress": Bingham *Ancestors' Brocade* 6; one dress preserved: Higgins 726, fn 516

2: "her habitual wearing": Bianchi, *Face to Face* 52

3: the other two poems are "Dare you see a soul at White Heat" and "A solemn thing – it was – I said – "; the first edition: Todd

4: consummation in heaven: Van der Vat 251-52

5: role model in "Aurora Leigh": Walker, *Approaches* 143; influence of Elizabeth Barrett Browning: Bogus 38-46

6: "to be a poet": Dietrich 97

7: "drama of self discovery": Crumley, "Self as Theme" 262

Chapter 21: The Gentleman Caller and the Maiden

1: *Because I could not stop for Death*: F479/J712; Cotton Mather burning her as a witch: Tate 13-14

3: "morality, piety ": First Church of Amherst, Congregational Church's Puritanism: Wolff 66

4: "Please, sir": *Letters* #153, 1:283

5: journey through youth, maturity and age: Anderson, "Emily Dickinson" '983-84, 1014; the ring as symbol of human cycle: Srinath 23; poet's own life-long fixation on death: Vendler 227-228

6: tippet defined as a lady's wrap: Bradbrook 600; "That obliging gentleman": England 79; examines grammar and tone: Porter 81

7: a special kind of burial vault: Abbott, "Dickinson's 'Because'" 140-43; sinking along with it her bodily remains: Vendler 228

9: "Flood subject": *Letters* #319, 2:454

10: "one of the greatest": Tate 13-14

11: pivotal role of fourth stanza: Christanne Miller, "'Because'" 14

12: an immortality of its own: suggested by Wolff 276

Chapter 22: Writing for Posterity

1: *This is my letter to the world* : F519/J441; "joy": *Letters* #963, 3: 857; "like immortality": *Letters* #330, 2:460; estimated 10,000 letters: Sewall 2:400; 1049 letters: *Letters*; drafts of poems and letters intermingled: Higgins 6-7

2: "I have written": *Letters* #30, 1:81

3: " there is another ": *Letters* #58, 1:149; also Johnson, *Poems* 4 (#2)

4: "I rise, because": *Letters* #172, 1:304; "I tie my": F#522; "The often complementary": Monteiro, "Business" 41

5: "supposed person": *Letters* #268

6: Frazar Stearns death: Habegger 400; "Austin is stunned": *Letters* #255, 2:397-98; "It feels a": F#524

7: fascicle with two other Civil War poems: Leder 3-5; also see Wolosky

10: Guerra 62-63

11: translated into many languages: Eberwein 164-65 ,92-93, 118-19, 258-59, 171-72

Chapter 23: Blotting Out the Light

1: *I heard a fly buzz when I died*: F591/J465; "Bye and bye": *Letters* #86, 1:197-98

2: "stole softly": *Letters* #11

4: "began with last": Hogue 26; "operates in terms . . ."; Anderson, *Stairway* 231-32

5: poem's great irony: Todd, *Persona* 68-69; theme is fraud: Pollak, *Dickinson* 193-98

6: "To live and": Johnson, *Letters* #184, 2:328

6: "We had such": *Letters* #142, 1:272; cited as possible germ of this poem: Sherwood 12

7: Mrs. Browning as a source: Capps 85-86; "The ear is": *Letters* #405, 2:518

8: Bible as source of Beelzebub, persona in hell: Hollahan 6

9: experience in the kitchen, housewives' abhorrence : Hogue 26; "putrefaction": Friedrich 35; "the fly's anticipation": Mudge 101

11: "The Ear is": *Letters* #405, 2:518

12: an ennobling gladness: *Letters* #356, 2:484; "Consciousness is the": *Letters* #591, 2:634

Chapter 24: Weighing the Brain

1: *The brain is wider than the sky* : F598/J632; "She had to think ": Bingham, *Home* 413-14

4: consciousness and God appear indistinquishable: Springer, "'The Brain is'" 281; "easy equivalency": Juhasz, *Undiscovered Continent* 26-27, 177

5: the "You" to whom the poem is addressed: Wolff 462; "watchfully by her subjective": Van Dyne 465-67, 468, 473

6: a creation of the human mind: McCarthy 31; "neither more nor less ": O'Connor 106;

7: "between the thing": Weisbuch 161-62, 195n; "God works through": Porter 98; "in intelligible Syllables": Vendler 17-18

8: makes her modern: Kirby 56-57; "Does God exist": Center for Spirituality and the Mind, www.uphs.upenn.edu/News_Release/April 25, 2006; Damasio, *The Feeling*

Chapter 25: The Insane Majority

1: *Much Madness is divinest Sense*: F620/J435; "Think Emily lost": *Letters* #234, 2:376; "Tell all the truth": F1263, See Chapter 30

5: "in thinking of ": *Letters* #7, 1:182

6: "The importance of": Habegger 176; Edward Dickinson's commitment to treatment for the insane: Habegger 411; "I want to have", Habegger 176

7: "a terror": *Letters* #261, 2:404; "I felt a Funeral", F340, See Chapter 15; "height of turmoil": Cody 294; "a snarl in": *Letters* #281, 2:424; "I felt a Cleaving": F867

9: "She is rather": Habegger 243

10: "my partially cracked": Sewall 1:6; "Oh why do": Sewall 1:6

12: "I think I was enchanted": F627; as tribute to Browning: Bogus 38-46

13: "Pardon my sanity": *Letters* #185, 2:329; "Insanity to the sane": *Letters* #209, 2:356; "discerning Eye" as key to poem: Nathan 36

Chapter 26: An Out-of-Body Seaside Walk

1 : *I started early – took my dog*: F656/J520; "I never saw": See Chapter 28

2: "has absolutely nothing": Weisbuch, "Prisming Dickinson" 204-205; a seaside description in her textbook: Capps 106-107

3: "a Dog – large": *Letters* #261 2:404; Carlo's name: Tingley 192; appears in over forty letters and poems: Freeman 41; "while the huge dog": Leyda 2:21; "my Carlo": *Letters* #34 1:92

4: "the traditional symbol": Winters 284; also Porter 99; symbolizes sexual love: Flores 47; also Khan 41

5: "a first enjoyable": O'Maley 86-88; "not entirely unwilling": Shurr 19-20; "erotics of heterosexual rape": Alfrey; "a sexual nightmare": Morey 12; "a study in": Flores 47; "superbly dramatic": Anantharaman 77-79

6: "The vast unconscious": Cody 306-07

7: "dramatization of the": Carlson 72

8: nature against culture: Kirkby, "Crisis" 57

9: loss of self-identity: Carlson 72

Chapter 27: Saying No to Life

1: *I cannot live with You* : F706/J640; Wadsworth as "Master": Shurr, 89-93

4: Wadsworth "Oceans" away: Habegger 444

6: "heartbreaking poem": Vendler 298

7: poem's pattern and narrative structure: Wolff 419-23

8: "I confess that": *Letters* #559, 2:614-15

9: "found Emily reclining": Leyda 2:375-76; "I do – do want": *Letters* #728, 3:66- 64

10: "by her hand": from T. W. Higginson's diary in Leyda 2:475

Chapter 28: Taking It on Faith

1: *I never saw a Moor*: F800/ 1052

2: "I am continually": Letters #10, 1:27;"Christ is calling": *Letters* #35, 1:94

3: "They are religious": *Letters* 261; "the Lord Jesus Christ" rivaled by Santa Claus: Sewall 1:269 (Apendix II);"promised Resurrection": Wolff 154-55 (in letter to her cousin, John Graves in April 1856)

4: See Chapters 2, 7, and 24 in this book

5: "I saw the sunrise": *Letters* #321, 2:455

6: interpreted as ironic: Greg Johnson 57-58; "critique of the values of her time": Merideth 448-51; "whistling in the dark": Griffith, *Long Shadow* 109-10, 139

7:"one of Dickinson's clearest": Monteiro, "Privileged" 48-49; "childlike faith in": Lair 13, 135; dynamic of hope and despair: Wolff 586 n.

8: "an experimenter of the spirit": Sewall, "Teaching" 38

11: follows Watts' meter: DeJong 153; second stanza identical in subject matter: Davidson 144-45; a counterpoint rather than a parody: England 91

12: faith in her imagination: DeJong 152; "the best of all women": Mertins 385; poets need not go to Niagara: Bingham, *Brocade* 322

Chapter 29: The Poet as a Boy

1: *A narrow Fellow in the Grass*: F1096/ J986; "When much in" : *Letters* #271, 2:415

2: "fictions . . .on the whole": *Letters* #31, 1:88

3: 229 poems: Franklin 639

5: the long "o": Guthrie, "Near Rhymes" 73

6: "extraordinary" knowledge of the Bible: Capps 41; "She knew every": Wolff 72

8: eight other poems: Vendler 396; "You know that pie": *Letters* #571, 2:622; according to Ned's sister: Bianchi, *Face to Face* 169; Uncle Emily: *Letters* #315, 2:4499: "How did that girl": Bianchi, *Face to Face* 2710: "free and fearless": Habegger 159

11: "Since the most powerful": Rich 49-74

12: publication history: Leyda 1:110-12, Sewall 2:476; "Lest you meet" : *Letters* #316, 2:450; "nearly caused a breach": Habegger 508

13: snake as a phallic symbol: Cody 437-38; bare feet: McQuire 84; sadomasochistic element: Scott 133

14: effect on the speaker: Judine 132-33

Chapter 30: Dimming Truth's Dazzle

1: *Tell all the truth but tell it slant*: F1263/J1129; *Rev. Jenkins' examination: Jenkins "Friend and Neighbor"*

4: "indirection and the unexpected": Eddy 266

5: cites Acts 9:4 of Bible: Wolff 153

6: God as the "omitted center": Lawson 24-27, 29

7: written in pencil on a fragment of stationery: *Franklin, Varorium Edition* 3:1089-90

Chapter 31: The Strongest Friends of the Soul

1: *There is no Frigate like a Book*: F1286/J1263; visits to optho-mologist in Boston: Hirschorn, "Medical Posthumous" 299-316; "a woe": *Letters* #439; also see Chapter 14

2: "Going home": Sewall, *Lyman Letters* 76

3: "Kinsmen of the Shelf": F#512; "This then is"(Higginson's account in a letter to his wife): *Letters* #342b, 2:475

5: 900 titles: Eberwein 27; references and allusions to authors: Capps; Howe; Pollak, "Literary Allusions" 54-68; Stonum 44-60; three pictures in her bedroom: Fuss 59

7: "A Book is": *Letters* #794, 3:756

Chapter 32: The Flash of the Hummingbird

1: *A Route of Evanescence*: F1489/J1463; fifty poems: Eberwein 22

2: sent to five friends: in addition to Helen Hunt Jackson and the Norcross cousins documented below, copies were sent to Sarah Tuckerman (*Letters* #627, 3:655); Thomas Higginson (*Letters* #675, 3:681) in 1880; and Thomas Niles (*Letters* #814, 3:769) in 1883

3: "I know your": *Letters* #601a, 2:638; "To the Oriole": *Letters* #602, 2:639-40

4: an allegory of the artist, "arrives like the bird": Vendler 479-481

5: "sustained metaphor": Sewall, "Teaching" 37; "gone before it": Daiches 727, n. 308; kinetic energy: Porter 76-77

6: source in Shakespeare's "Tempest": Frank Davidson 407-08; similar to a mailman: Allen 52-54

7: For details of the love affair between Austin Dickinson and Mabel Todd, see Polly Longsworth, *Austin and Mabel*

8: "I know not": *Letters* #769, 3:740; Emily listened from upstairs: Higgins 216

Chapter 33: The Lure of the Simple Life

1: *How happy is the little Stone*: F1570/ J1510; "You are a":
Johnson *Letters* #444a, 2:545

2: "'H. H.'once told": *Letters* #749b, 3:726

3: "The kind but": *Letters* #749, 3:725

5: "I often wish ": *Letters* #182, 2:324

6: a metaphor for her life: Lair 165 and Anderson 164; a recluse
writing at home: Morey, "Hundred Best" 165; "The little
stone's": Durnell 19-20

7: "I am small ": *Letters* #268, 2:411

8: "indifference of ": Kimpel, "Dickinson as Philosopher" 197-98;
"harmony and integration": Kher, "'An Abyss's Face'" 12-14

9: lacks freedom: Olpin, "Hyperbole: Part One" 15; "the trouble is":
Robinson 76

9: logic behind her concept: Wilson, "Problem of Career" 455-56.

Chapter 34: God's Little Blond Blessing Gone

1: *Pass to thy Rendezvous of Light* : F1624/J1564; "willful and
winsome": Bianchi, *Face to Face* 172

2: "God's little Blond": *Letters* #589, 2:633

3: "Gilbert asked a": *Letters* #711, 3:701; "to carry to": *Letters*
712, 3:701; " Poor Little Gentleman": *Letters* #754 3:732

4: "His fever was": *Letters* #868, 3:799;:Sewall, 1:146

5: 'Open the Door': *Letters* #873, 3:802-03

6: "Gilbert rejoiced in": *Letters* #868, 3:799

7: "I see him" and " He knew no": *Letters* #868, 3:799

8: "wronged only of" and "to see him": *Letters* #868, 3:799

9: "Requiem ecstasy": *Letters* #868, 3:799

10: "alarmingly ill for" Sewall 1:146; "Nervous Prostrations": *Letters*
#873, 3:802-03; never recovered completely: Higgins 226-
27

11:"Biography first convinces": *Letters* #972, 3:863-64; Dickinson's
use of elegy: Rizzo 105

Chapter 35: The Blond Assassin at Play

1: *Apparently with no surprise*: F1668/J1624

2: an envelope addressed to Aunt Elizabeth Currier: Farr, *Passion* 116

3: "I remember he": *Letters* #692, 3:693

4: a fever epidemic in Amherst: Farr, *Passion* 116; "I can't stay": *Letters* #195, 2:341

5: "When Flowers annually": *Letters* #488, 2:573

Chapter 36 The Final Confrontation

1: *My life closed twice before it's close*: F1773/J1732 : "tremulous fear": Bingham, *Home* 4; "cut to the heart": Habegger 407

2: See Chapter 3 for details of the three early losses.

3: The five subsequent "losses" are documented in all the standard biographies of Dickinson. "His heart was": Sewell 1:55, 2:486; Samuel Bowles as "Master" supported by Sewall, Wolff, and Farr; Charles Wadwsorth as "Master" supported by Habegger and Pollak; twenty-one letters to the Clark brothers: Farr in Eberwein 302; last one during her own final days: *Letters* #1040 3:901; Emily's grief over Gib's death: See Chapter 34; "The Dyings have": *Letters* #939 3:843

4: "Eight Saturday noons": *Letters* #907 3:826-27

8: "full barrenness of human fate": Woolf 148; "sentimental, spiritual," "entirely clear": Woolf 534. A notably different interpretation is given by Vendler who views the three "events" in the poem as identical: "Death, Death, Death": Vendler 520. Others have interpreted Emily's so-called "last words" differently. For example, Habeggar sees them as inconclusive, part of Dickinson's "riddling" which he deemed "as strong and light-hearted as ever": Habeggar 626.

9: "Called Back": *Letters* #1046

10: description of Dickinson's gravesite: Longsworth, *World* 113

Bibliography

Abbott, Collamer M. "Dickinson's 'Because I could not stop for Death.'" *Explicator* (2000) 58: 140-43.

————. "Safe in their Alabaster Chambers." *Explicator* (2000) 60:139.

Alexander, Charlotte. *The Poetry of Emily Dickinson.* (Monarch Notes, No. 00780) New York: Monarch Press, 1965.

Alfrey, Shawn. *The Sublime of Intense Sociability:Emily Dickinson, H.D., and Gertrude Stein.* Bucknell, 2000.

Allen, Mary. *Animals in American Literature.* Urbana: U of Illinois P, 1983.

Anderson, Charles R. "Emily Dickinson." *In American Literary Masters.* By Charles R. Anderson, et al. New York: Holt, Rinehart and Winston, 1965. 1:965-1032.

————. *Emily Dickinson's Poetry: Stairway of Surprise.* New York: Holt, Rinehart and Winston, 1960.

Ando, Midori. "Birds." In Eberwein 22-23.

Anonymous. "The Newest Poet." *London Daily News* (2 January 1891).

Bennett, Paula. "Flowers." In Eberwein 115-16.

————. "Jewels." In Eberwein 166-167.

Benfey, Christopher. "'Best Grief is Tongueless": Jerome Liebling's Spirit Photography." In *The Dickinsons of Amherst.* Hanover and London: UP of New England, 2001.

Bianchi, Martha Dickinson. *Emily Dickinson Face to Face: Unpublished Letters with Notes and Reminiscences by Her Niece.* Boston, Houghton Miflin, 1932.

————. *The Life and Letters of Emily Dickinson.* Boston: Little Brown, 1924

————, ed. *The Single Hound: Poems of a Lifetime.* Boston: Little Brown, 1914.

Bingham, Millicent Todd. *Ancestors' Brocades: The Literary Debut of Emily Dickinson.* New York and London: Harper Brothers, 1945.

————. *Emily Dickinson's Home: The Early Years as Revealed in Family Correspondence and Reminiscences.* New York: Dover Publications, 1955.

Biscella, Susan. "Civil War." In Eberwein 46-47.

Bogus, S. Diane. "Not So Disparate: An Investigation of the Influence of Elizabeth Barrett Browning on the Work of Emily Dickinson." *Dickinson Studies* 49, 1(1984): 38-46.

Bouson, J. Brooks. "Emily Dickinson and the Riddle of Containment." *Emily Dickinson Bulletin*, no. 31 (First Half 1977): 33-49.

Bradbrook, M. C. "Review of Anderson and Ward." *Modern Language Review*, 57, no 4 (October 1962): 599-600.

Brooks, Cleanth, R. W. B. Lewis, and Robert Penn Warren, eds. *American Literature: The Makers and the Making.* New York: St. Martins Press, 1973.

Cambon, Glauco. "Emily Dickinson and the Crisis of Self-Reliance." In *Transcendentalism and Its Legacy.* Myron Simon and Thornton H. Parsons, eds. Ann Arbor: Michigan UP, 1966.

Cameron, Sharon. *Choosing Not Choosing: Dickinson's Fascicles.* Chicago: U of Chicago P, 1992.

Capps, Jack Lee. *Emily Dickinson's Reading 1836-1886.* Cambridge: Harvard UP, 1966.

Carlson, Eric W. "'I started early – took my dog – .' " Explicator (May 1962): Item 72.

Challiff, Cynthia. "The Bees, the Flowers, and Emily Dickinson," *Research Studies* (Washington State Univ.), 42, no. 2 (June 1974): 93-103

Clapp-Itnyre, Alisa. "George, Eliot." In Eberwein 98-99.

Cody, John. *After Great Pain: The Inner Life of Emily Dickinson.* Cambridge: Harvard UP, 1971.

Crumbley, Paul. "Dickinson's Dialogoc Voice." In Grabher 93-109.

————. "Self, as Theme." In Eberwein 262.

Cunningham, J. V. "Sorting Out: The Case of Emily Dickinson." *Southern Review*, n. s. 5, no. 2 (Spring/April 1969), 436-56.

Daiches, David and William Charvat, eds. *Poems in English, 1530-1940.* New York: Ronald Press, 1950.

Damasio, Antonio. *The Feeling of What Happens: Body and Emotion in the Making of Consciousness*. New York: Harcourt, 1999

Dandurand, Karen. "Drum Beat." In Eberwein 89.

Davidson, Frank. "A Note on Emily Dickinson's Use of Shakespeare." *New England Quarterly*, 18 (1945):407-08.

————. "Emily Dickinson and Isaac Watts." *Boston Public Library Quarterly*, 6, no. 3 (July 1954): 141-49.

Davis, Thomas M., ed. *14 by Emily Dickinson with Selected Criticism*. Chicago: Scott Foresman, 1964.

Day, Martin S. *A Handbook of American Literature*. St. Lucia: U. of Queensland Press, 1975.

deFord, Sara. "Emily Dickinson," in *Lectures on Modern American Poetry*. Tokyo: Hokuseido Press, 1957, 1-26.

Dietrich, Deborah. "Election, as Theme." In Eberwein 96-97.

DeJong, Mary. "Hymns, Influence of." In Eberwein 152-53.

Dietrich, Deborah. "Election as Theme." In Eberwein 96-97.

Duncan, Jeffrey L. "Joining Together/Putting Asunder: An Essay on Emily Dickinson's Poetry." *Missouri Review* 4.2 (Winter 1980-81): 111-29.

Durnell, Hazel B. *Japanese Cultural Influences on American Poetry and Drama*. Tokyo: Hokuseido P, 1983.

Eberwein, Jane Donahue. *An Emily Dickinson Encyclopedia*. Westport CT, London: Greenwood Press, 1998.

Eddy, Sara. "Slantness." In Eberwein 266-67.

England, Martha Winburn. "Emily Dickinson and Isaac Watts: Puritan Hymnodists." *Bulletin of the New York Public Library*, 69, no. 2 (February 1965):83-116.

Faderman, Lillian. "Emily Dickinson's Homoerotic Poetry." *Higginson Journal*, no. 18 (1st Half 1978): 19-27.

Farr, Judith. *The Passion of Emily Dickinson*. Cambridge: Harvard UP, 1992.

————. *The Gardens of Emily Dickinson*. Cambridge: Harvard UP, 2004.

Fast, Robin Riley and Christine Mack Gordon. *Approaches to Teaching Dickinson's Poetry*. New York: Modern Language Association, 1989.

Faulkner, Howard. "Emily Dickinson." *Critical Survey of Poetry: English Language Series.* Frank N. Magill, ed. Englewood Cliffs NJ: Salem, 1982.

Fegan, James and Haruko Kimura. "Insects." In Eberwein 160.

Ferlazzo, Paul J. *Emily Dickinson.* Boston: Twayne, 1976.

First Church of Amherst. *Articles of Faith and Government.* Amherst MA, 1834

Flores, Kate, "Dickinson's 'I Started Early – Took My Dog.'" *Explicator* 9 (May 1951): Item 47.

Ford, Thomas W. "Emily Dickinson and the Civil War." *University Review* 31 (1965): 199-203,

Frankenberg, Lloyd. *Invitation to Poetry.* Garden City NY: Doubleday, 1956.

Franklin, R. W. *The Editing of Emily Dickinson: A Reconsideration.* Madison: U of Wisconsin P, 1967.

————. *The Manuscript Books of Emily Dickinson.* Cambridge: Harvard UP, 1981.

————. *The Master Letters of Emily Dickinson.* Amherst, MA: Amherst College Press, 1986.

————. *The Poems of Emily Dickinson.* Cambridge: Harvard UP, 1999.

————. *The Poems of Emily Dickinson, Variorum Edition.* 3 vols. Cambridge: Harvard UP, 1998.

Freeman, Margaret. "Carlo." In Eberwein 41.

Friedrich, Gerhard. "Dickinson's 'I heard a fly buzz when I died.'" *Explicator* 13, no. 6 (1955): Item 35.

Fry, August J. "Writing New Englandy: A Study of Diction and Technique in the Poetry of Emily Dickinson. In *From Cooper to Philip Roth: Essays on American Literature.* J. Bakker and D.R. M. Wilkinson, eds. Amsterdam: Rodopi, 1980. 21-31.

Fuss, Diana. *The Sense of an Interior: Four Writers and the Rooms that Shaped Them.* Routledge, 2004.

Galperin, William. "A Posthumanist Approach to Teaching Dickinson." In Fast 113-17.

Garbowsky, Maryanne M. *The House without the Door: A Study of Emily Dickinson and the Illness of Agoraphobia.* Rutherford NJ: Fairleigh Dickinson UP, 1989.

Gordon, Lyndall. *Lives like Loaded Guns: Emily Dickinson and her*

Family Feuds. Viking Books, 2010.

Grabher, Gudrun, Roland Hagenbuchle and Cristanne Miller. *The Emily Dickinson Handbook.* Amherst: U of Massachusetts P, 1998.

Griffith, Clark. "Emily and *Him*: A Modern Approach to Emily Dickinson's Love Poetry." *Iowa English Yearbook.* No. 6 (Fall 1961): 13-22.

Griffith, Clark. *The Long Shadow: Emily Dickinson's Tragic Poetry.* Princeton NJ: Princeton UP, 1964.

Guerra, Jonnie. "Dance Responses to Dickinson." In Eberwein 62-63.

Guthrie, James R. "Measuring the Sun: Emily Dickinson's Interpretation of Her Optical Illness." *Emerson Society Quarterly* 41 (1995): 239-55.

————. "Near Rhymes and Reason: Style and Personality in Dickinson's Poetry." In Fast 70-77.

Habegger, Alfred. *My Wars Are Laid Away in Books: The Life of Emily Dickinson.* New York: Random House, 2001.

Hamada, Sahoko. "Consciousness, as Theme." In Eberwein 55-56.

Hart, Ellen Louise and Martha Nell Smith, ed. *Open Me Carefully: Emily Dickinson's Intimate Letters to Susan Huntington Dickinson.* Ashley MA: Paris Press, 1998.

Hecht, Anthony. "The Riddles of Emily Dickinson." *New England Review* (Autumn 1978): 1-24.

Higgins, David. *Portrait of Emily Dickinson: The Poet and Her Prose.* New Brunswick, NJ: Rutgers UP, 1967.

Hirschhorn, Norbert and Polly Longsworth. "Medicine Posthumous: A New Look of Emily Dickinson's Medical Conditions." *New England Quarterly* 69 (June 1996): 299-316

Hockersmith, Thomas E. "'Into Degreeless Noon' : Time, Consciousness, and Oblivion in Emily Dickinson." *American Transcendental Quarterly* 3.3 (Sept. 1989): 277-95.

Hogue, Caroline. "Dickinson's 'I heard a fly buzz when I died'" *Explicator* 20 (November 1961): Item 26.

Hollahan, Eugene. "Dickinson's 'I heard a fly buzz when I died.'" *Explicator* 25, no. 1 (1966): Item 6.

Howe, Susan. *My Emily Dickinson.* Berkeley, CA:North Atlantic Books, 1985.

Jenkins, MacGegor. *Emily Dickinson: Friend and Neighbor.* Boston: Little Brown, 1930.

Johnson, Greg. *Emily Dickinson: Perception and the Poet's Quest.* U of Alabama P, 1985.

Johnson, Thomas, ed. *The Complete Poems of Emily Dickinson.* Boston: Little Brown, 1960.

————. *Emily Dickinson: an Interpretive Biography.* Cambridge: Harvard UP, 1955.

————, ed. *The Letters of Emily Dickinson.* 3 vols. Cambridge: Harvard UP, 1965.

————. "Textual Notes: 'Safe in their Alabaster Chambers.'" In Davis 19-23.

Jones, Rowena Revis. "Congregationalism." In Eberwein 53-54.

Judine, Sister M. Judine, I. H. M. "Whitman and Dickinson." *In The Teacher and American Literature.* National Council of Teachers of English, 1965.

Juhasz, Suzanne. "'I Dwell in Possibility': Emily Dickinson in the Subjunctive Mood." *Emily Dickinson Bulletin*, no. 32 (Second Half 1977):105-09.

————. *Naked and Fiery Forms: Modern American Poetry by Women, a New Tradition.* New York: Octagon. 1976.

————. *The Undiscovered Continent: Emily Dickinson and the Space of the Mind.* Bloomington: Indiana UP, 1983.

Jumper, Will C. "Dickinson's 'The Soul Selects Her Own Society.'" *The Explicator* 29, no. 1 (September 1970), Item 5.

Keller, Karl. *The Only Kangaroo Among the Beauty: Emily Dickinson and America.* Baltimore: Johns Hopkins UP, 1979.

Kemp, Carolyn. "Renunciation, as Subject and Strategy." In Eberwein 246-47.

Khan, Salamatullah. *Emily Dickinson's Poetry: The Flood Subjects.* New Delhi: Aarti Book center, 1969.

Kher, Inder Nath. "'An Abyss's Face': The Structure of Emily Dickinson's Poems." *Pluck*, 2, no. 1 (Fall 1968), 12-14

Kher, Inder Nath. *The Landscape of Absence: Emily Dickinson's Poetry.* New Haven: Yale UP, 1974.

Killingsworth, M. Jimmie. "Whitman and Dickinson." *American Literary Scholarship: An Annual 2001.* Durham, London: Duke UP, 2003.

Kirkby, Joan. *Emily Dickinson.* New York: St. Martin's Press, 1991.

————. "Crisis." In Eberwein 56-57.

Knapp, Bettina L. *Emily Dickinson.* New York: Continuum, Frederick Ungar, 1989.

Kurjiaka, Susan. "Romanticism." In Eberwein 251-53.

Lackey, Allen D. "Dickinson's *I Never Lost As Much But Twice.*" *The Explicator,* 34, no. 3 (November 1975), Item 18.

Lair, Robert L. *Barron's Books Notes: A Simplified Approach to Emily Dickinson.* Woodbury NY: Barron's Educational Series, 1971.

Lambert, Robert. "This is Radio Kuwait – In the Words of the Poet Emily Dickinson: An American Voice." *Higginson Journal of Poetry,* 3. no. 6 (First Half 1973), 13-18.

Lawson, Elizabeth. "Emily Dickinson: a slant on immortality." *Dickinson Studies,* no. 56 (2d Half 1986): 24-37.

Lease, Benjamin. "Colloqualism." In Eberwein 49-50.

――――. "Higginson, Thomas Wentworth." In Eberwein 139-41.

Leder, Sharon with Andea Abbott. *The Language of Exclusion: The Poetry of Emily Dickinson and Christina Rossetti.* Contributions in Women Studies, no. 83. New York: Greenwood, 1987.

Lewis, R. W. B. "Foreword." In Wolff xvii-xxx.

Leyda, Jay. *The Years and Hours of Emily Dickinson.* 2 vols. New Haven: Yales UP, 1960.

Longsworth, Polly. *Austin and Mabel.* Farrar, Straus, Giroux, 1984.

――――. "The 'Latitude of Home": Life in the Homestead and the Evergreens." *In The Dickinsons of Amherst.* Hanover and London: UP of New England, 2001.

――――. *The World of Emily Dickinson: A Visual Biography.* New York: Norton, 1990.

Lucas, Dolores Dyer. *Emily Dickinson and Riddle.* Dekalb: Northern Illinois UP, 1969.

Luscher, Robert T. "An Emersonian Context of Dickinson's "The Soul selects her own Society." *ESQ: A Journal of the American Renaissance* 30 (2nd Quarter 1984): 111-16.

McCann, Janet. "Ambiguity." In Eberwein 3-4.

McCarthy, Paul. "An Approach to Dickinson's Poetry." *Emerson Society Quarterly,* no. 44 (Third Quarter 1966): 22-31.

McDermott, John F. "Emily Dickinson's 'Nervous Prostration' and Its Possible Relationship to Her Work." *Emily Dickinson Journal* 9:71-86.

McIntosh, James. *Nimble Believing: Dickinson and the Unknown.* Ann Arbor: Michigan UP, 2000.

McNeil, Helen. *Emily Dickinson.* New York: Pantheon; London: Virago, 1986.

McGuire, Mary Ann C. "A Metaphorical Pattern in Emily Dickinson." *American Transcendental Quarterly*, no. 29, pt. 2 (Winter 1976):83-85.

Machor, James. "Emily Dickinson and the Feminine Rhetoric." *Arizona Quarterly*, 36.2 (Summer 1980): 131-46

Malbone, Raymond G. "Dickinson's 'I taste a liquor never brewed.'" *Explicator*, 26. no. 2 (October 1967):Item 14.

Marcus, Mordecai. *Emily Dickinson: Selected Poems.* Lincoln, NE: Cliff Notes, 1982.

Martin, Wendy. *An American Triptych: Anne Bradstreet, Emily Dickinson, Adrienne Rich.* Chapel Hill: U of N. Carolina P, 1984.

Merideth, Robert. "Emily Dickinson and the Acquisitive Society." *New England Quarterly*, 37 (December 1964):448-51

Mertins, Louis. *Robert Frost: Life and Talks–Walking.* Norman: U of Oklahoma P, 1965).

Miller, Cristanne. "'Because I could not stop for Death—.'" In Eberwein 13-15.

————. "Approaches to Reading Dickinson." *Women's Studies* (1989): 223-28.

————. "Disjunction, as a Characteristic." In Eberwein 84-86.

Miller, James E., Jr. *Quests Surd and Absurd.* Chicago: U of Chicago Press, 1967.

Mitchell, Domnhall. "The Train, the Father, His Daughter, and Her Poem: A Reading of Emily Dickinson's 'I like to see it lap the Miles.'" *Emily Dickinson Journal* 7, i, 1-26.

Monteiro, George. "Dickinson's Select Society." *Dickinson Studies*, no. 39 (1981):41-43.

————. "Emily Dickinson's Business." *Literature and Belief*, 10 (1990):24-42.

————. "Privileged and Presumptuous Guests: Emily Dickinson's Brazilian Translators." Luso-Brazilian Review, 8, no. 2 (Winter 1971):39-53, 48-49.

————. "Traditional Ideas in Dickinson's "I Felt a Funeral, in my Brain." *Modern Language Notes*,74, no. 8 (December 1960): 656-63.

Morey, Frederick L. "Hundred Best Poems of Emily Dickinson." *Emily Dickinson Bulletin*, no 27 (First Half 1975): 4-49.

————. "The Fifty Best Poems of Emily Dickinson." *Emily Dickinson Bulletin*, no. 5 (First Half 1974): 5-23.

Mossberg, Barbara Antonina Clarke. *Emily Dickinson: When a Writer Is a Daughter.* Bloomington: Indiana UP, 1982.

Mudge, Jean McClure. *Emily Dickinson and the Image of Home.* Amherst: U. of Massachusetts P, 1975.

Nathan, Rhoda. "'The Slanted Truth: Thoreau's and Dickinson's Roles." *Thoreau Journal Quarterly* 11.3/4 (July-Nov. 1979):35-40.

Oberhaus, Dorothy Huff. "Dickinson as Comic Poem." In Fast 118-123.

O'Connor, William Van. *The Grotesque: An American Genre and Other Essays.* Carbondale: Southern Illinois UP, 1962.

O'Maley, Carrie. "'I Started Early – Took My Dog –.' " *Explicator* (2003) 61: 86-88.

Paglia, Camille. *Sexual Personae: Art and Decadence from Nefertiti to Emily Dickinson.* New Haven CT: Yale UP, 1990.

Perkins, James A. "A History of Explication of P 1052: 'I never saw a Moor — ." *Dickinson Studies* 63 (2d Half 1987): 30-32

Perrine, Laurence. "Critical Commentary: 'There's a certain Slant of light.'" In Davis 34-35.

Phillips, Elizabeth. *Emily Dickinson: Personae and Performance.* University Park: Pennsylvana State UP, 1988.

Pickard, John B. *Emily Dickinson, An Introduction and Interpretation.* New York: Barnes and Noble, 1967.

Pollak, Vivian R. *Dickinson: The Anxiety of Gender.* New York: Cornell UP, 1984.

————. "Emily Dickinson's Literary Allusions." *Essays in Literature,* I (1974): 54-68

————. *A Historical Guide to Emily Dickinson.* New York: Oxford UP, 2004

————. 'That Fine Prosperity': Economic Metaphors in Emily Dickinson's Poetry." *Modern Language Quarterly*, 34, no. 2 (June 1973): 161-79

Porter, David T. *The Art of Emily Dickinson's Early Poetry.* Cambridge: Harvard UP, 1966.

Raab, Josef. "The Metapoetic Element in Dickinson." In Grabher 273-95.

Rao, J. Srihari, ed. *Essential Emily Dickinson.* Bara Bazar B: UP Praksh Book Depot, 1972.

Reed, Michael. "Masculine Identity and Oral Security in the Poetry of Emily Dickinson." *Journal of Evolutionary Psychology* 9.3-4 (1988): 278-86.

Rich, Adrienne. "Vesuvius at Home: The Power of Emily Dickinson." *Parnassus: Poetry in Review*, 5, no. 1 (Fall-Winter 1976), p. 49-74.

Rieke, Susan. ""Some keep the Sabbath going to Church –." In Eberwein 267-68.

Rizzo, Patricia Thompson. "The Elegaic Modes of Emily Dickinson." *Emily Dickinson Journal* 11 (2002) 1:104-17.

Robinson, John. *Emily Dickinson: Looking to Canaan.* Faber Student Guides. London: Faber, 1986.

Salska, Agnieszka. "Emily Dickinson's Lover." In *Studies in English and American Literature.* Warsaw: Polish Scientific Publishers, 1984. 135-40.

Savage, D. S. "Death: A Sequence of Poems." In *Master Poems of the English Language.* Ed. Oscar Williams. New York: Trident Press, 1966. 750-55.

Scholnick, Robert J. "'Don't Tell! They'd Advertise': Emily Dickinson in the *Round Table.*" *Periodical Literature in Nineteenth-Century America* 166-82.

Scott, Wilbur S. *Skills of the Poet.* New York: Harper and Row, 1977.

Sewall, Richard B. *The Life of Emily Dickinson.* 2 vols. New York: Farrar, Straus, & Giroux, 1974.

————. *The Lyman Letters: New Light on Emily Dickinson and Her Family.* Amherst: U of Massachusetts P, 1965.

————. "Teaching Dickinson: Testimony of a Veteran." In Fast 30-38.

Sherwood, William R. *Circumference and Circumstance: Stages in the Mind and Art of Emily Dickinson.* New York: Columbia UP, 1968.

Short, Bryan C. "Aphorism." In Eberwein 9-10.

Shullenberger, William. "My Class had stood – a Loaded Gun." In Fast 95-104.

Shurr, William H. *The Marriage of Emily Dickinson: A Study of the Fascicles.* Lexington: UP of Kentucky, 1983.

Spear, Lynne EFM. "'There's a certain Slant of Light.'" In Eberwein 283-84.

Springer, Haskell. "'Much Madness is divinest Sense —.'" In Eberwein 200.

————. "The Brain – is wider than the Sky—." In Eberwein 281.

Srinath, C. N. "The Poetry of Emily Dickinson: Some First Impressions." *Literary Criterion,* 9, no. 1 (Winter 1969):19-28.

St. Armand, Barton Levi. "Keeper of the Keys: Mary Hampson, the Evergreens, and the Art Within." In *The Dickinsons of Amherst.* Hanover and London: UP of New England, 2001.

————. *Emily Dickinson and her Culture: The Soul's Society.* Cambridge: Cambridge UP, 1984.

Stewart, Randall. *American Literature and Christian Doctrine.* Baton Rouge: Louisiana State UP, 1958.

Stonum, Gary Lee. "D's Literary Background." In Grabher 44-60.

Tate, Allen. *Reactionary Essays on Poetry and Ideas.* New York: Charles Scribner's Sons, 1936.

Thackrey, Donald E. "Critical Commentary: 'There's a certain Slant of light.'" In Davis 35-37.

Tingley, Stephanie A. "Marvel, Ik." In Eberwein 191-92.

Todd, John Emerson. *Emily Dickinson's Use of the Persona.* The Hague: Mouton, 1973.

Todd, Mabel Loomis and Thomas Wentworth Higginson, eds. *Collected Poems of Emily Dickinson: Poems,* 1890; *Poems, Second Series,* 1891; *Poems, Third Series,* 1896. Boston: Roberts Brothers.

Towheed, M. Q. "The Wit of Emily Dickinson." *Banasthali Patrika,* No. 11 (July1968) 20-30,

Stephenson, William E. "Emily Dickinson and Watts's Songs for Children." *English Language Notes,* 3, no. 4 (June 1966) 278-81.

Taggard, Genevieve. "I taste a liquor never brewed'; Critical Commentary." In *14 by Emily Dickinson with Selected Criticism.* Thomas M. Davis, ed. Chicago: Scott Foresman, 1964. 13-14.

Van der Vat, D. G. "Emily Dickinson (1830-1886)." *English Studies*, 21 (1939):241-60.

Van Dyne, Susan R. "Double Monologues: Voices in American Women's Poetry." *Massachusetts Review* 23.3 (Autumn 1982): 461-85.

Walker, Cheryl. "A Feminist Critic Responds to Recurring Student Questions about Dickinson." In Fast 142-47.

Walker, Julia M. "Emily Dickinson's Poetic of Private Liberation." *Dickinson Studies*, no. 45 (June 1983): 17-22.

Walker, Nancy. "Emily Dickinson and the Self: Humor as Identity." *Tulsa Studies in Women's Literature* 2 (1983) 57-68.

———. "Voice, Tone, and Persona in Dickinson's Love Poetry." In Fast 105-06.

Wallace. Ronald. *God Be with the Clowns: Humor in American Poetry*. Columbia: U of Missouri P, 1984.

Wegelin, Christof. "Dickinson's 'Wild Nights.'" *The Explicator*, 26, no. 3 (November 1967): 25.

Weisbuch, Robert. *Emily Dickinson's Poetry*. Chicago: U of Chicago P, 1975.

———. "Prisming Dickinson, or Gathering Paradise by Letting Go." In Grabher 197-223.

Westbrook, Perry D. *Free Will and Determinism in American Literature*. Rutherford NJ: Fairleigh Dickinson UP, 1979.

Whicher, George Frisbie. *This Was a Poet, A Critical Biography of Emily Dickinson*. New York: Scribner's, 1938.

Wilbur, Richard. "Sumptuous Destitution." In *Emily Dickinson: A Collection of Critical Essays*. Ed. Judith Farr. Prentice-Hall, 1996. 53-61.

Wineapple, Brenda. *White Heat: The Friendship of Emily Dickinson & Thomas Wentworth Higginson*. New York: Knopf, 2008.

Winters, Yvor. *In Defense of Reason*. Denver: Alan Swallow, 1947.

Wolff, Cynthia Griffin. *Emily Dickinson*. New York, Knopf, 1986.

Wolosky, Shira. *Emily Dickinson: A Voice of War*. New Haven: Yale UP, 1984.

❧ Alphabetical Listing of Poems ❦

❧ About the Author ❧

*L*ea Newman earned a Ph.D. in American literature at the University of Massachusetts at Amherst and is Professor Emerita at the Massachusetts College of Liberal Arts. She has written books on Hawthorne and Melville and is Past President of both the Hawthorne and the Melville societies. She was a Fulbright scholar in residence at the University of Bologna and the University of Urbino in Italy and has written essays on Dante's influence on Melville and on Florence as a source for Hawthorne's "Italian" novel *The Marble Faun*. She is also the author of a memoir, *Growing Up Italian in Chicago*, and of the award-winning book *Robert Frost: The People, Places, and Stories Behind His New England Poetry*. She currently serves as Vice-President of the Friends of Robert Frost and is a founder of the Robert Frost Stone House Museum in Shaftsbury, Vermont, not far from Bennington, where she has lived for the past forty-five years. She has taught Emily Dickinson's poetry during her more than three decades in the college classroom and has spent the past seven years researching Dickinson's life and poetry in the light of her teaching experience.

More Praise for

Emily Dickinson

"Virgin Recluse" and Rebel: *36 Poems, Their Backstories, Her Life*

There is a compelling and beautiful integrity in every word that Lea Newman has written here. She takes Emily Dickinson's poems in her hands and reveals the human light that illuminates each one. The result is at once eye-opening and shrewd without missing anything hidden within Dickinson's most personal works. Newman's insight is up to the challenge and each story throws new light on even the most familiar verses. How lucky for any reader to discover this long-awaited guide to Dickinson's world."

Bill Morgan, author of
I Celebrate Myself: The Somewhat Private Life Of Allen Ginsberg

"Lea Newman's "Virgin Recluse and Rebel" is a wide- ranging yet concise in-troduction to the poetry and life of Emily Dickinson, a compellingly organized, incisive intro-duction to the work of one of our greatest writers. This guide in-troduces us to three dozen of her best poems (out of 1789) and in orderly fash-ion introduces us to "the back- story" of each text. A concise feast of delights, blooming with insights and valuable juxtapositions among the poems."

Stephen Sandy, author of
The Thread, New and Selected Poems.

"Focusing on a careful and skillful selection of Emily Dickinson's poems in the context of a close and dedicated reading of the poet's letters, a combing of con-temporary and latter-day reminiscences, and an incorporation of the insights of dedicated scholars since Dickinson's posthumous debut in the 1890 Poems, this intelligent and passionate book will take you through many of most revered poems in the Dickinson canon as well setting you on some unfamiliar paths through the poet's intriguingly simple but ever mysterious life."

George Monteiro, author of
The Experienced Emblem: A Study of the Poetry of Emily Dickinson

"A lively and engaging volume that welcomes readers into Dickinson's world and works."

Karen Kilcup, author of
Nineteenth-Century American Women Writers

"Lea Newman's essays on a representative selection of Dickinson's poems pro-vide an excellent overview of the range, power, and relevancy of this great writer's work. Though intended as an introduction to Dickinson's poetry, those readers more familiar with Dickinson will be rewarded as well by Newman's lively, observant, and well-written analyses."

David Garnes,
Dickinson scholar, writer, lecturer, and reviewer

CPSIA information can be obtained at www.ICGtesting.com
Printed in the USA
BVOW08s0632130214

344797BV00001B/21/P